KEMPEITAI

Japan's Dreaded Military Police

RAYMOND LAMONT-BROWN

SUTTON PUBLISHING

First published in 1998 by
Sutton Publishing · Phoenix Mill
Thrupp · Stroud · Gloucestershire · GL5 2BU

ISBN 0-7509-1566-8

 ALAN SUTTON™ and SUTTON™ are the
trade marks of Sutton Publishing Limited

Typeset in 11/13 pt Bembo.
Typesetting and origination by
Sutton Publishing Limited.

CONTENTS

I am now convinced that it was mainly the worst elements within the Japanese Army who were assigned military police [Kempeitai] duties. The autocratic authority they exercised was quite unbelievable in relation to their responsibilities. In sharing conclusions with other Allied officers, I am left in no doubt as to the evil pervading their sadistic ranks. So far as Allied prisoners were concerned, God help them if captured or placed in the custody of the Kempeitai. Instances of mindless brutality and beheadings were widespread throughout the Japanese Army and were pursued in complete disregard of the Geneva Convention or justice to the point, or so it would seem, that genocide was part of the Japanese conquering agenda.

However and above all, the Kempeitai were evil personified. Instances of bestial torture and inhuman acts outweighing what Japanese troops perpetrated in the field – if that was possible, were carried out by the Kempeitai. Time and time again I have encountered conflicting testimony apportioning blame in the defence of 'no responsibility'. Either, the Kempeitai were a law unto themselves, or had the tacit consent of superior officers. Whatever, I would have to acknowledge that these same members of the Kempeitai, stripped of their authority and weapons, are a pathetic but devious lot. The junior ranks are included in this description but with the observation that many of them are of low intelligence and can lie against all odds, making even the devil smile in evil admiration.

Personal notes, March 1948, by Captain James Gowing Godwin (1923–95), Australian Army Intelligence (2nd War Crimes Section)

CHRONOLOGY

1936

25 Nov.   Imperial Japanese Ambassador Extraordinary and
           Plenipotentiary, *Shishaku* Kintomo Musha-no-koji signs
           Rome-Berlin-Tokyo (Axis) agreement to guard against
           International Communism.

1937

6 Nov.   Anti-International Communism Protocol signed by
           Axis countries.

1940

1 Aug.   Japanese cabinet declare policy of 'New Order' in
           Greater East Asia.

27 Sept.   Ten-Year Pact signed between Axis countries at Berlin
           for establishment of 'New Order'.

1941

26 Jan.   *Gaimu-daijin* Yosuke Matsuoka reiterates Japanese claims
           in the Pacific.

4 Apr.   Matsuoka discusses with Hitler possibility of attack on
           Singapore and war with US.

28 Jul.   UK and US assets frozen in Japan.

17 Oct.   *Sori-daijin* Hideki Tojo forms new cabinet.

18 Nov.   Japanese Diet passes 'resolution of hostility' to US.

7 Dec.   Japanese attack on Pearl Harbor.

8 Dec.   Japan declares war on UK & US (at 6 a.m., Tokyo time).

1942

27 Feb.   Battle of the Java Sea.

4 May   Battle of the Coral Sea.

4 Jun.   Battle of Midway Island.

1 Sept.	Japanese *Gaimusho* assumed by Hideki Tojo on resignation of Shigenori Togo. Ministry of Greater East Asia set up in Tokyo.

1943

9 Feb.	Japanese evacuate Guadalcanal.
2 Mar.	Battle of the Bismark Sea. Heavy Japanese losses.
8 Oct.	Hideki Tojo takes over as *Shoko-daijin*.

1944

25 Feb.	Japan withdraws from Burma.
5 Jul.	Japan suffers losses, New Guinea.
18 Jul.	Hideki Tojo resigns as *Sori-daijin* and Chief-of-Staff. Cabinet changes show an escalating desire to end the war. Hard-liners talk of 'stronger measures'.
23 Aug.	Japanese fighting forces driven out of India.
23 Oct.	Second battle of the Philippines; Japanese fleet routed.

1945

25 Feb.	US occupy Manila.
1 Apr.	US 10th Army invades Okinawa.
3 May	Rangoon captured.
5 Jul.	General MacArthur announces the liberation of the whole of the Philippines.
15 Aug.	V-J Day.
16 Aug.	Emperor Hirohito orders all troops to cease fire.
1 Sept.	Japanese Unconditional Surrender signed aboard the USS *Missouri*, in Tokyo Bay, by *Gaimu-daijin* Mamoru Shigemitsu.
2 Sept.	Japanese envoys sign surrender at Manila.
5 Sept.–24 Oct.	Sequence of Japanese surrenders from SW Pacific to Burma.
Dec.	'Major' war crimes trials begin in Manila. Followed by Tokyo Trials.

ACKNOWLEDGEMENTS

People

'The Kempeitai were without doubt the elite of the Japanese military forces. In Japan any member of the Kempeitai was saluted by army personnel with meticulous correctness. When a member of the Kempeitai was within sight of civilians, no matter how far away, the civilians went down on their knees and then bowed with their faces only an inch or two from the ground. And they stayed in that position until the Kempeitai was completely out of sight.'

Thus are the Kempeitai remembered by such as former Private of the 8th Division Australian IF, Roy H. Whitecross who was a PoW of the Japanese during 1942–5. The author is grateful to him, and to the many such former victims of the Kempeitai, who have contributed personal backgrounds to help tell the story of the infamous Japanese military police. The author also wishes to thank the following, particularly, for assisting in preparing and researching the text: Charlie Smith of the BCAIR Japan Association; Arthur Lane, National Ex-Servicemen's Association; L. Ball of the Commonwealth War Graves Commission; Neil Griffiths, the Royal British Legion Scotland; Miss Fujiko Kobayashi, Japan/Korean Librarian SOAS; Maj. A. Black, SFEPOW; Prof. Ian Nish; Ms Waheeda Abdur Rahun, National Parks Board, Singapore; Secretariat, Burma Star Association and Masafume Kikuta of the National Institute for Defence Studies, Tokyo; Sok-Cheng Tay, the *Straits Times*, Singapore; and Ann Levick of the Association of

ACKNOWLEDGEMENTS

British Civilian Internees, Far East Region. And to the ex-PoWs like my friend of many years James Alan Ford, CB, MC.

Text

Each quotation is individually acknowledged as it occurs in the text. Special thanks are given to the following for helping trace rights ownership and specific quotations: Lionel Leventhal, of Greenhill Books for *Handbook on Japanese Military Forces*; Catherine Trippett of Reed Books for *Japanese All* by J. Ingram Bryan; Betty R. Weston of Robert Hale Ltd for *Bamboo and Bushido* by A.G. Allbury; Penny Coles of HarperCollins Publishers for *Prisoner of Japan* by Phyllis Argall; and to Roy H. Whitecross for quotations from his book *Slaves of the Son of Heaven* and in private correspondence with the author. Thanks go to William Hodge & Co. for textual quotations from the summing up of Lt-Col. S.C. Silkin in the trial of *Chusa* Haruzo Sumida. And to the estate of Lord Russell of Liverpool for *The Knights of the Bushido*.

Photographs

Each photograph is individually acknowledged where it occurs for source and ownership. Particular thanks, however, are due to S.A. Guild for supplying rare photographs of the Saigon–Cholan Kempeitai and giving permission for their use.

Documentation

On Japan's surrender on 15 August 1945 Kempeitai officers all over the Occupied Territories and the Japanese homeland destroyed the majority of their files. Curiously, this was also an act continued by the US Occupation Forces under, some historians say, a direct order of General Douglas MacArthur. Nevertheless files on the trials of

ACKNOWLEDGEMENTS

Kempeitai personnel may be found in the following archive locations: Philippine National Archives, Manila (including affidavits, statements and written evidence); National Archives, Washington, DC; National Diet Library, Tokyo; National Library Board, National Reference Library, Singapore; in the Indexes of the Public Record Office, Kew, UK; the Imperial War Museum, London; and in the National Archives of Australia and New Zealand.

It is worth noting that anniversaries of battle campaigns, often mentioned in the media, bring to light new material. For instance, in the General Government National Archives, Netherlands East Indies section, at the Hague, eyewitness reports were noted on the 'Kempeitai Pig Basket Atrocities'. It appears that in 1942, at East Java, many Dutch, US, British and Australian PoWs were slaughtered by the Kempeitai in 'pig baskets'. The PoWs were pushed into these bamboo baskets (used for transporting pigs to market) and thrown into the shark-infested waters of the Java Sea. Other baskets, it is believed, were doused in petrol and set alight.

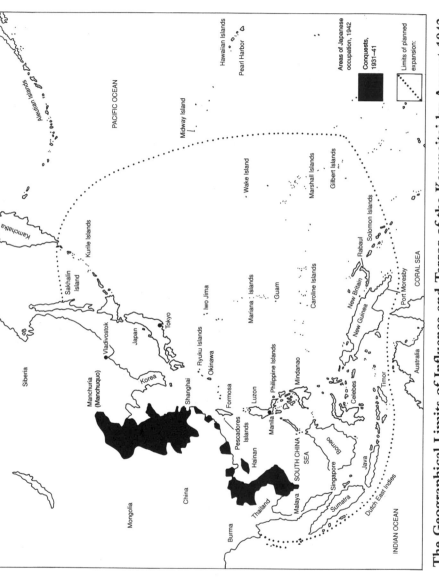

The Geographical Limits of Influence and Terror of the Kempeitai by August 1942

In under six months, following the devastating air attack on 7 December 1941 on Pearl Harbor, the US base in the Hawaiian Islands, by the naval forces of Taisho Isoroku Yamamoto, the Imperial Japanese Army and Navy had seized what it had taken the colonial powers several centuries to acquire. More than 1 million square miles of land in South-East Asia came under Japan's jurisdiction, with 150 million people, plus half a million European and US civilians and 150,000 prisoners.

FIRST ENCOUNTERS WITH THE KEMPEITAI

The world I knew is now a shameful place.
There will never come a better time
For me to die.

Poem by Taisho *Tomoyuki Yamashita (1885–1946),*
hanged as a Class A
War Criminal

The Chamber of Commerce, Saigon . . . Pudu Jail, Kuala Lumpur
. . . Outram Road, Singapore . . . all locations seared into the
memory of those who encountered the Kempeitai during the
Second World War, for each was the site of a military police
headquarters where unspeakable horrors were inflicted on human
beings; sometimes for the only reason that they were *gaijin.* My
own first encounters with the Kempeitai were through the pages
of my late father's diary. He had been a prisoner of the Kempeitai
during the early 1940s in Shanghai, East China. The
psychological scars of that brush with them never healed and
shortened his life, as such treatment did for thousands of innocent
people.

Most travellers to Shanghai in those days came upon the city
by ship up the foetid waters of the Huangpu River. Following

Refugees flood into Shanghai's International Settlement as the Imperial Japanese Army closes in. Here at Garden Bridge over Soochow Creek, at its junction with the Huangpu River by Broadway Mansions, was the boundary between the Japanese and British sections of the International Settlement. The Kempeitai had headquarters on the city's Bund (waterfront) and the notorious Bridge House Prison. (Japan Research Projects – JRP).

the Treaty of Nanking (1842), which opened Shanghai to foreign trade, the river was a route taken by the colonial gunboats and foreign opium traffickers to the Bund, the internationally famed Shanghai waterfront. Here European, American and Japanese colonial powers had built one of the first commercial enclaves in China. In the 1920s and 1930s Shanghai was known by some as the 'Paris of the Orient', and by others as 'the Whore of the East'.

Shanghai was China's most westernised city with thoroughfares with names like Park Lane and Avenue Edward VII. The British had their clubby, horsey concession here from 1843 and met each other at such watering places as the Shanghai Club which boasted the world's longest bar. Here, too, gathered the agents of the world's powers to glean gossip to repeat at their chancelleries. The Americans, who joined the British ex-pats to form the International Settlement in 1863, met up in such places as Jimmy's Kitchen, where the best coffee in the Orient was deemed to be dispensed. Adjacent was the French Concession of 1849, taking in leafy streets and *maisons tolérées* (as the brothels were known), and its atmosphere of Roman Catholic mission. Into this melting pot came some 20,000 White Russians fleeing from Bolshevism and later European Jews escaping from National Socialism. Each of the city's foreign zones had its own armed and police forces and court systems, and none was more rigorous in its efficiency and paranoia than the Kempeitai.

During the 1930s the Japanese government worked on their plans to dismember China, and their reign of terror in Manchuria led to a huge upsurge in anti-Japanese feeling so that by 1931, the Chinese were boycotting Japanese goods. In Shanghai the anti-Japanese feelings were particularly strong because the Japanese population formed the largest foreign group in the International Settlement. On 21 January 1932 the Japanese Consul General demanded the Chinese Mayor of Greater Shanghai, General Wu Te-chen, to suppress all anti-Japanese sentiment, and punish the culprits who had killed Japanese citizens in the recent riots.

Before the mayor was to deliver a 'meek and submissive' reply, *Chujo* Koichi Shiozawa, Commander of the Japanese Yangtze Squadron launched an attack on 28 January. This was to form the first 'Shanghai Incident'. Rapidly the Japanese occupied the city's Cha'-p'ei section and an aerial bombardment commenced. Fierce fighting ensued between General Ts'ai T'ing-k'ai's 19th Route Army and the Japanese forces, but at last the Chinese withdrew. A truce of sorts was signed in May 1932 through the intercession of the British government and the League of Nations. Japanese expansion in China continued, and by 1935 the five northern provinces of China were within a zone of intense Japanese influence. Effectively China was under the control of the two Japanese commanders *Taisho* Hisaichi Terauchi and *Taisho* Kenkichi Ueda, and in their command were hundreds of Kempeitai personnel.

Soon the Japanese were to embark on their 'Shanghai Campaign' and in August 1937 the killing of two Japanese mercenaries near Shanghai led to a full-scale invasion. On 2 December 1937, 6,000 Japanese soldiers took part in a victory parade in Shanghai, which now became an occupied city. Through December 1937 to October 1938, the Japanese took Hsuchou, Canton and Wuhan and in March 1940 the Japanese established a puppet government under the Chinese Nationalist defector Wang Ching-wei at Nanking. Meanwhile life went on in the International Settlement, deals were struck, contracts signed and my father continued with his civil engineering work for the Anglo-Scottish company of Babcock & Wilcox Ltd, boilermakers of Renfrew.

When Japan declared war on the US and UK on 8 December 1941 the Kempeitai and the Japanese forces commandeered all property and set up barbed wire barricades all over Shanghai. The Kempeitai established themselves at a headquarters on the Bund

Rare photograph of a Kempeitai patrol boat cruising the Huangpu River, Shanghai. The vessel flies the Hinomaru sun ray flag which the military sported during the Second World War. (JRP)

and at what was to be the notorious Bridge House Prison. At the time my father was a resident of the Palace Hotel. In his diary he left a record of his arrest by the Kempeitai under the date 5 March 1942:

The real shock came to me personally this morning at 4am [the Kempeitai liked to make their arrests at 0300hrs Tokyo time], when I was rudely awakened by five plain clothes Kempeitai, four of whom, in true gangster fashion, were brandishing revolvers. The fifth Kempeitai officer, who carried a light machine gun, ordered me to get up and dress. Meanwhile, the other four were making a thorough search of all my belongings. At the conclusion of the search, I found that two of my cases had been filled with [anti-Japanese] papers and certain books. I was then forced to accompany the Kempeitai, carrying my cases, to a waiting car. Apparently the Kempeitai were taking no chances, as all five armed men accompanied me on the journey. I was very careful not to make any false step, fully realising what this would undoubtedly mean. The car pulled up at a large building, which I recognised as the dreaded 'hell-hole' of Shanghai, officially termed 'Bridge House Prison'. I was roughly bundled out of the car and upstairs to a room containing a varied assortment of nationalities, all caught in the drag net laid by the invader.

After about two hours, I was ordered to take everything out of my pockets, take off my collar, tie, braces and [sock] suspenders. I was at a loss to understand why I was suddenly being treated as a criminal, and while I was being hurried across the prison yard, I endeavoured to obtain an explanation from one of the Kempeitai. The only response was a horrible growl, as I was thrust into a wooden cage, and the gates closed behind me.

On entering the cage, the first thing that struck me was the terrible smell, which I found to my disgust came from an unscreened wooden sanitary bucket, in the corner, which was being used by men, women and children of all nationalities.

The problem was now to adapt myself to living without shoes to keep my feet warm, and braces to keep up my trousers. . . .

[6 March 1942]
The next morning, after a sleepless night on a concrete floor without blankets, I was taken out of this cage together with three

other men, and escorted to another cage, in an old section of the place, where conditions were even worse. This cage was about 9 ft 4 in by 20 ft, and the same horrible smell pervaded the place. The cage contained a mixture of Chinese, Russians, Americans and British. During my period there, up to 42 persons were in the cage at one time, making it necessary for a certain number to sleep in a sitting posture, when sleep could be had. Often sleep was rudely disturbed by a new arrival, or someone being taken out for interrogation.

As with all Kempeitai prisons interrogations went on in Bridge House all the time. And every hour somewhere someone was screaming with the pain of torture, untended wounds or sheer terror. As the hours went by my father tried to take his attention off the horror of the place by figuring out mathematical problems, recalling conversations he had had with friends and chronicling his childhood in the Scottish Border Country. Time passed with no real memory of its passing and slowly people became dehumanised and just caged carcasses. My father continued his story thus:

. . . so many of the Chinese in this cage were suffering from horrible diseases – in fact some stank of rotting flesh – [this] added to the horror of the situation. There was a constant fear that the disease might be carried to us by vermin, and I considered myself extremely lucky to have escaped contracting any of these diseases, as quite a number of white people were not so fortunate. As a matter of fact, a well-known journalist in the same cage as myself lost both feet.

For food we had nothing other than boiled rice, the smell of which was positively nauseating. No change of food was allowed until I had been interrogated, and it was twenty-four days before I was allowed to wash and shave, and I was even prevented from having a change of clothing. The charge against me was one of espionage and propaganda. . . .

After brutal interrogation to no avail my father was released and was repatriated aboard the *Kamakura Maru* and the SS *Narkunda* with other British citizens.

Historians endeavouring to research Japanese Second World War studies in general, and Kempeitai activities in particular, have long come across the two main ethnic characteristics to thwart their success: namely, 'Tactical Myopia' and 'Strategic Amnesia Syndrome'. For decades the *Gaimusho* have had a blinkered attitude to such events as *Taisho* Iwane Matsui, Commander-in-Chief of the Central China Area Army's 'Rape of Nanking' on 13 December 1937, in which 300,000 Chinese nationals were slaughtered and maimed, and actively discouraged all who sought to build up a picture of Japan's role in the Second World War. Only since the 1990s has the *Mombusho* allowed new textbooks to give anything like detailed accounts of the Second World War from any point of view. Although shrines and temples in Japan blatantly display memorials to dead Kempeitai officers, there is a national forgetfulness when one makes enquiries about the careers of these 'honourable dead', and one is likely to receive a platitude in reply like *Anna hito-bito wa kuni no meiyo desu* ('Such men are a great honour to their country').

This book attempts to give the first real examination in English of the overall history of the Kempeitai, their organisation and methods. Throughout it is a tale of harrowing scenarios. A look at the possible reasons why the Kempeitai committed such deliberate cruelties and exhibited such disregard for human suffering might be useful for a western audience, without in any way condoning anything the Kempeitai did. Clues lie in the structure of Japanese society, its past military codes and its conception of humanity.

The abuse of PoWs in the history of warfare has been, and remains, a universal problem. As Japan emerged from feudal purdah in the nineteenth century, the nation's proclivity to racial discrimination – that is, a subscription to the view of all nations as inferior to the *Kami*-country of Japan – was hardened into *gaijin* being considered sub-human by the new military ideology suffused throughout Japan from around the annexing of Korea in 1910. From the time of the Sino-Japanese War (1894–5), a Japanese soldier was expected to commit suicide rather than surrender. This was the ideology known as *gyokusai*, which led to the implementation of the *kamikaze* air and sea attacks of the Second World War. This latter ethic applied as a strategy (as opposed to a spontaneous act) was one of the reasons why surrendering Allied troops and personnel were held in such contempt by the Japanese – they had lost face before the enemy. Further, the Imperial Army Military Training regulations stimulated a modern reconstruction of *Bushido* ('The Way of the Warrior'), the ancient military code of conduct. As Article 2 of the regulations stated: 'The duty of the military is to sacrifice their lives for the Emperor's country. It is a tradition inherited from the time of the old *samurai*. A *samurai*'s loyalty to his country has been considered even more important than the worth of his own life.' Hence the Japanese believed that surrendering PoWs had lost all honour and loyalty to their beliefs. It must be said that the Kempeitai in particular corrupted what was the fine military code of *Bushido* with its five main tenets of righteousness, courage, humanity, propriety and sincerity. PoWs believed that because of *Bushido* they were harshly treated, but *Bushido* in its original form never condoned cruelty, the Kempeitai made it a travesty.

Up to the end of the Second World War the Japanese attitude to human rights was one of indifference, and a theoretical acceptance of the concept dated only in statute from the first state constitution (the Meiji Constitution of the Great Japanese Empire; which remained in force until 1947) of February 1889. Even so, all constitution articles were capable of being over-ridden by the letter of the law. This is evident from just one example: Article 29 stated, 'Japanese subjects shall, within the limits of the law, enjoy the liberty of speech, writing, publication, public meetings and associations.' In reality this was not to be so, and the Kempeitai in particular were to help nullify the whole of Article 29 in their role as 'thought police' along with the TOKKO.

Duty of the citizens of Japan to emperor and motherland always outweighed any personal rights. It was the duty, for instance, of citizens to bear the consequences of Japan's defence machine. Thus when the ammunition dump at Itabashi, Tokyo, blew up severely damaging nearby private property, the government refused to pay compensation as it was the duty of the dump's neighbours to bear any danger for the good of the country's defence. As all Japanese were brought up to recognise blind duty to one's superiors and, ultimately, to the emperor, all military orders were considered to be in his name. Consequently, an order to execute, torture or mistreat PoWs was deemed an imperial command to be carried out without hesitation.

Human worth in Japan was very much dependent upon one's status in society. As society was a pyramid of classes in Japan, with the emperor and his family at the top and the *burakumin* (untouchables) at the bottom, each person was judged by his or her place in the pyramid system. As PoWs were thought to be sub-human (i.e. below the *burakumin* because they were *gaijin*), they were not considered to have any human worth, or human rights.

From the founding of the Imperial Japanese Army in 1902, its structure contained the potential for brutality. Japanese soldiers were ill-treated by their superiors (at all rank levels) as a matter of course. Discipline included *bentatsu* (beatings) to underline orders; so the slapping of PoWs – or anyone, for that matter – by soldiers, even for the most trivial of instructions not carried out, was an accepted commonplace set within a lawful military frame.

It will be noticed, too, that as the Kempeitai began to lose confidence in their powers to maintain security in the Occupied Territories, their cruelties increased in direct proportion. This situation was worsened as the war began to go badly for the Japanese. The Kempeitai became more suspicious, aggressive and paranoid as the Allies moved nearer to the homeland; and Kempeitai arrests and tortures escalated. It is also true that Kempeitai cruelties were a form of revenge for territories lost, and enhanced the illusion of dominance in Occupied Territories remaining. Some even talk of Kempeitai torture being 'therapeutic' − aiding the psychological well-being of the perpetrators.

CHAPTER ONE

ROOTS OF THE KEMPEITAI

*[The Kempeitai were a] grimly efficient corps . . . possessing wide powers
and trained to employ those powers ruthlessly.*

Lionel Wigmore, The Japanese Thrust *(1957)*

I The Development of the Police Force

Japan's contemporary police system is called *keisatsu*. This is a
mixture of the centralised and totalitarian police structure of the
pre-Second World War era – from which the Kempeitai evolved
with such power – with the decentralised local police units of the
days immediately following the Japanese surrender to the Allies
aboard the battleship USS *Missouri* in Tokyo Bay on 2 September
1945.

In the decades before the Edo period (1603–1868) of Japanese
history, society was formally controlled fundamentally by the
military. The *samurai* (warrior) class and the *kebiishi* (the ancient
police department) were supplemented by groups of citizens
organised collectively for mutual protection. During the Edo
period, the *Shogun* (the generalissimos who ruled Japan in the name
of puppet emperors) – dominated by the Tokugawa family –
evolved an elaborate police system. The chiefs of the police were
the *machi bugyo* (town magistrates of *samurai* class), who acted as
prosecutors and judges in criminal matters in Edo (later to become

the capital city of Tokyo) and the power bases of the castle-towns of Japan. These magistrates were assisted by *metsuke* (inspectors) who were nothing less than secret police who ferreted out supposed corruption and misrule among officials; they also spied upon individuals and groups who were considered to be a danger to the government.

The everyday responsibilities of these magistrates were delegated to the horse-mounted *yoriki* and the foot-patrol *doshin* (literally 'companions' – police sergeants and ordinary ranks), who were also of *samurai* class. The lowest rung of policing was carried out by *meakashi* (detectives: *okappiki* in Edo parlance) who carried *jitte* (short metal truncheons) to counter the swordplay of criminals. Quite often the *meakashi* were former criminals who, intent on self-preservation, had avoided execution by swearing loyalty to the *Shogun*. In several of the countries occupied by the Japanese during the Second World War the Kempeitai made use of criminals and outlaws as law enforcers.

Within the private, rural domains of the *Shogun*, policing was carried out by 'local intendants' known as *daikan*. And the *Shogun's* direct control of society was augmented by citizens' mutual responsibility organisations (i.e. the *Goningumi*, 'Five-family associations') of friends and neighbours who took collective responsibility for good behaviour of their members to the government.

On 3 January 1868 a new Imperial Government was proclaimed which effectively brought to an end the rule of the *Shogun*. Henceforth the country was directly ruled by the Emperor Meiji (*r.* 1868–1912), who yanked Japan out of its existence as a feudal state into the modern world. As a consequence, the modern Japanese army with its cornerstone of conscription was established (1872) and police organisation was reviewed.

One Toshiyoshi Kawaji was now sent to Europe in 1872 to prepare a study of contemporary police systems. When he returned in 1873 he recommended a programme of measures for police reorganisation, mainly based on the police systems of France's Third

Republic and the Prussian methods of Kaiser Wilhelm I's Germany. Kawaji became head of the *Keishicho* (Tokyo Metropolitan Police Department) in 1874. In parallel, Imperial Japanese Army officer students were dispatched around the world to study army systems, and particularly to Germany, where Prussian militarists impressed the Japanese government.

In 1873, too, the *Naimusho* (Home Ministry) was established which controlled the administration of Japan's prefectures through appointed governors. In 1871 the old feudal domains had been abolished and the country divided into *ken* (prefectures). The *Naimusho* controlled police through the *Keihokyoku* (Police Bureau), delegating routine management of police activities to the prefectures. By 1875 the *Gyosei Keisatsu Kisoku* (Administrative Police Regulation) separated police law enforcement from judicial functions which were now the responsibility of the *Shihisho* (Ministry of Justice, later to be called the *Homusho*). The police, however, retained authority to deal with quasi-judicial functions and to issue ordinances.

The Japanese police had a wide range of duties which went far beyond the functions of crime prevention, protection of life and property, the arrest of criminals and the maintenance of public peace. They regulated everything from public health to factory construction, from issuing permits for a wide range of activities to controlling businesses. When fighting broke out in China in 1937, the stringencies of war added responsibilities to the police mandate to include such functions as motivating labour and controlling transportation. They also had the duties of social censorship on all branches of the media (within the press law of 1875), as well as the monitoring of political activities, particularly concerning *shukai jorei* (public meetings).

The *Tokubetsu Koto Keisatsu* (TOKKO – Special Higher Police – colloquially translated, the 'thought police'), founded in 1901 as the civilian counterpart to the Kempeitai, were to make full use of the legislation regarding the *shukai jorei*. Their particular targets were those in such meetings suspected of 'political crimes', and teachers and society leaders who were deemed possessed of 'dangerous thoughts'.

In 1932 the TOKKO were divided into six departments: special police work, with two offices for political activities; *gaijin* (foreigner) surveillance – ordinary citizens were accosted for reading foreign language books, and houses were broken into if agents heard music being played that was by foreign composers; labour relations; Koreans in Japan; censorship; and arbitration. Throughout the 1930s the prime groups targeted by the TOKKO and Kempeitai were students, farmers, socialists, communists, pacifists, foreign workers and any showing irreverence for the emperor. The TOKKO had offices in Shanghai, London and Berlin.

The TOKKO enforced the many security laws, particularly the National Defence Security Law (6 March 1941) and the New Peace Preservation Law (8 May 1941), both of which gave them and the Kempeitai a legitimate *carte blanche* to pry into every aspect of individuals' lives – and administer 'justice'. Their work was greatly enhanced by the setting-up of the *Tonari Gumi* (Neighbourhood Associations). These were divided into branches by street, block and building, each branch reporting to a co-ordinator who in turn reported to the TOKKO (and, where relevant, the Kempeitai). The intrusive presence of the *Tonari Gumi* was considered a national scandal, for in 1930 the newspaper *Mainichi Shimbun* commented: '[the groups amount] to a national spying system, of sneaking into each other's houses and reporting them to the police. This system will afford the malignant means to injure others against whom they may happen to have some grudge.'

All house servants were a part of the *Gumi* network, and some reported directly to the Kempeitai whose records displayed some of the farcical aspects of the 'dangerous thoughts' system. Writing in *Collier's Magazine* (27 October 1945), the US correspondent F.D. Morris quotes one servant saying to his employer (on a particularly quiet day in the household): 'Please give me a piece of paper with something – anything – written on it. I have to make a report to the Kempeitai today.' The *Japan Times* noted that between 1933 and 1936 some 59,013 people had been arrested for harbouring 'dangerous thoughts' by the TOKKO and Kempeitai; some 5,000 were brought to trial, and some 2,500 were given prison sentences.

Persons arrested for 'dangerous thoughts' were ordered to write their autobiographies, and comment on how they had arrived at their political/ideological opinions. The autobiography system was to be a common task set for prisoners by the TOKKO and Kempeitai during the Second World War, particularly for foreign correspondents and supposed spies. If the suspects did not compose what the TOKKO or Kempeitai wanted to read, they were ordered to do the composition again. It was a no-win situation; if the suspects wrote what the interrogators expected, they were charged with having committed a political crime.

A TOKKO arrest usually conformed to a pattern, and was vividly remembered by the film-director Akira Iwasaki. It was a cold winter's night when he was arrested, recalled Iwasaki; three TOKKO, all dressed in black, turned up at his Tokyo residence without warning. He was hauled out of bed. While he was dressing the agents ransacked the house for books, diaries, scripts and documents and he was then taken to Ikebukuro police station in north-west Tokyo. Before TOKKO officials began interrogation he was warned that he would be severely punished for not confessing – to what was not clear. Iwasaki was held prisoner for fourteen months; at length he was released with the warning to refrain from political expression or activity.

The Kempeitai themselves were well established before the TOKKO, having been founded by order of the Meiji Council of State of 4 January 1881, as an élite corps of 349 men. Their first work was to discipline army officers who resisted conscription. They not only 'policed the army' but regulated the people as well; for farmers also protested against the conscription law which took

16

young men from the rice fields. Under the Acts of 1898 and 1928 the Kempeitai functioned in a General Affairs Section and a Service Section. The former concerned itself with policy, personnel, discipline and records and took on the duties of the TOKKO within the *Dai Nippon Teikoku Kaigun* (Imperial Japanese Navy) and the *Dai Nippon Teikoku Rikugun* (Imperial Japanese Army). The latter section was responsible for three main functions: the supply, organisation and training of police units; security; and counter-intelligence. There are mentions, too, in the 1920s of a section called the TOKKO-Kempeitai which dealt with what was termed 'anti-ideological work'.

In peacetime the Kempeitai were responsible to the *Rikugunsho* (Ministry of War) for normal military duties, to the *Naimusho* for civil police duties and to the *Shihisho* for law administration. As the regular police were far less numerous than today, officers of the Kempeitai assisted in the prefectures. Thus through the period 1898 to 1945 the Kempeitai were able to build up a huge network of influence and became omnipresent in the area of the *Dai Nippon Teikoku* (Empire of Great Japan) and the Occupied Countries of the *Dai Toa Kyozonken* (Great East Asia Co-Existence Sphere – the Japanese euphemism for their occupied territories). It was in the pursuit of *chian iji* (maintenance of order) that the Kempeitai first won their unsavoury reputation.

Overall, the Kempeitai formed a branch of the *Rikugun* via the *Heimu Kyoku* (Military Administration Bureau) under the leadership of a Provost Marshal General directly answerable to the *Rikugunsho*. In war/fortress zones they came under the command of the commanders of these areas, and in Manchuquo, Chosen and Formosa (the occupied territories of Manchuria, Korea and Taiwan) they answered to the commanders-in-chief of the areas. Throughout they were called upon, too, to assist local civilian law authorities. It is also important to stress, and this despite the use of the word in 1930–45 press reports, that the Kempeitai were never a gendarmerie.

17

Military/secret police structure with moral, spiritual and political links to the emperor as a god and commander-in-chief, and the Japanese war machine by 1944.

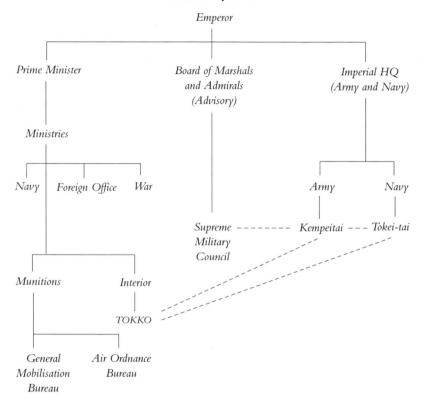

In no other country was the ordinary man and woman so in awe of the *keikan* (policeman) or the Kempeitai functionary. They were the visible arm of the law, the guardians of the law, the public censors and overseers of private morals and thought as well as arbiters of decorum. All prisoners of the regular police and the Kempeitai were presumed guilty on arrest and examinations of suspects took place in secret; the conception of *habeas corpus* (the individual's right to have his or her case tried before a court) was not recognised, and the use of torture to extract confessions of guilt was the rule of thumb. Officially torture was illegal in Japan when the Kempeitai were rising to great power, yet, as Professor J. Ingram Bryan pointed out in his *Japanese All* (1928; one of the first assessments in English of Japanese police methods): '[torture for] eliciting confessions in criminal cases is believed to be still practiced, because of the official conviction that no Oriental can be expected to tell the truth except under torture'. Many of the Kempeitai personnel learned their torture techniques when on civilian duty. Professor Bryan summarised the 1920s torture methods used by the *keikan* in training:

> The most common forms of torture are: suspending the body from a beam by a cord tied to the middle finger, the toes just touching the floor; or suspending the body by the wrists. A severer form is to tie the hands behind the back and then let the body hang by the hands from the beam, which almost disjoints the shoulder blades. Another way is to enclose the body in a box that presses in tightly on all sides, and then pour water on the face until the verge of suffocation is reached; also touching the body repeatedly with red hot irons, or pricking the body with sharp splinters; causing the victim to kneel and then placing over the ankles a piece of timber on either end of which stands a [*keikan*], almost dislocating the ankle joints. Twisting the joint of an arm to the point of dislocation is a common form of terrorising a victim into admission of guilt. Some prisoners have affirmed that they were beaten on the head until almost unconscious; and women became physical wrecks, if they do not die.

Otto D. Tolischus, correspondent for the *New York Times* and *The Times* of London, reported in his book *Tokyo Record* (1943) that at the outbreak of war, and while he was still an active journalist in Japan, he was arrested (as were all non-diplomat aliens) and tortured by the metropolitan *keikan* during the period 7–19 January 1942. This was in a clear attempt to make him confess to spying, the *keikan* tactics including face slapping and stamping on knees and ankles while the prisoner was in a kneeling position.

There was then an accepted use of torture in police matters which had official sanction and which was to be enacted in the armed forces with the knowledge and tacit approval of the *Sambo Hombu* (Imperial General Staff). The Kempeitai were to be the consummate torturers of the Second World War and their use of torture and human degradation was probably unsurpassed since the days of the Spanish Inquisition. Torture methods were on the syllabuses of the Kempeitai training schools and were thus sanctioned by the *Rikugunsho*. Wherever they held sway, from labour camps to occupied townships, the Kempeitai indulged in flogging, water torture by flooding the lungs, burning, scalding, electric shock treatment, knee joint separation, suspension (linked with flogging), kneeling on sharp edges, finger- and toe-nail removal and digit fracturing. Many Kempeitai officers invented their own tortures.

In terms of motivation the Kempeitai were known for their extraordinary discipline, and for their racial and political fanaticism. As one contemporary correspondent noted, they fought 'The Holy War for the Liberation of a Billion Asians'. As to work, the Kempeitai retained a very strong policing element and were rarely seen as field combat units except in counter-espionage forays. Again, their predominant role was to develop as camp police (in Indonesia in particular). The Kempeitai also had their own word for 'severe punishment without martial law intervention, leading to execution'; this was *kikosaku*. Thus it was not unusual for a Kempeitai officer to be police investigator, prosecutor, judge, jury and executioner. Against a Kempeitai charge there was no appeal for clemency and no civil help.

II Japanese Secret Intelligence

The Kempeitai were to have an important function in Japanese espionage and counter-intelligence as they evolved alongside and within Japan's other, nineteenth-century, intelligence services. When Japan abandoned its 'closed door' policy of isolation – for by the 1850s western nations were clamouring for trade and general commercial intercourse – they transformed their medieval feudal state into a modern nation. The policies now adopted made an espionage system essential.

From 1868 to 1945 Japan's international activities followed three basic tenets:

1. Japan is the centre of the world, with its ruler, the *Tenno* (emperor), a divine being, who derives his divinity through ancestral descent from the great Amaterasu-Omikami, the Goddess of the Sun herself.
2. The *kami* (Japan's pantheon of gods) have Japan under their special protection. Thus the people and soil of *Dai Nippon*, and all its institutions, are superior to all others.
3. All of these attributes are fundamental to the *Kodoshugisha* (Imperial Way) and give Japan a divine mission to bring all nations under one roof, so that all of humanity can share the advantage of being ruled by the *Tenno*.

Out of these tenets developed the philosophy of *Hakko Ichiu* ('The Whole World Under One Rule' – i.e. Japanese domination). The third tenet was to lead Japan into wars which targeted the nations that stood between Japan and the hegemony of the Orient. On 25 July 1894 Japan attacked China, leading to the naval defeat of China in the Battle of the Yalu River, and the massacre of Chinese at Port Arthur; a peace treaty was ratified with Japan as victor on 8 May 1895. War between Russia and Japan in Manchuria, Korea and the Chinese seas broke out in

1904 to end with Japanese victory and the favourable Treaty of Portsmouth in August 1905. Japan was now a major player on the international stage and an espionage system became an immediate necessity.

By the 1870s Japan was not exactly ignorant of espionage. Under the *Shoguns* a system of agents had worked to keep an eye on disaffected aristocrats and would-be rebels. As early as the Kamakura period (1185–1333), the *Shoguns* had used *ommitsu* (a general word for secret agents), often disguised as merchants, priests and fortune tellers; but they were only employed irregularly. With the coming of the Tokyugawa *Shoguns* these agents became more universally deployed in a variety of roles from *ninja* ('invisible agents') to *niwaban* (attendants who supervised the shogunate gardens). Now an agents' network was evolved to be used by the *Shoguns* for spying on the *daimyo* (feudal lords), who in turn spied on the *roju* (senior administrators), *metsuke* and *wakadoshiyori* (junior councillors).

There had been agents sent, too, to China to monitor that vast nation then sinking into chaos. In terms of modern espionage though, Japan was beginning from scratch and was in a position to be selective as to which system it might espouse. The Japanese have never been exponents of original thought. Their culture is basically Chinese at root, filtered through Korea in the baggage train of Buddhism; yet they became consummate improvers of the ideas of others, and the best espionage system that they could see in the 1870s was Germany's.

Japan's international spy network began in the early 1880s alongside the fledgeling Kempeitai. Their role model was to be the Prussian secret service expert Wilhelm Stieber (1818–92). A Saxon from Merseburg, Stieber had first studied theology and then law and became a criminal lawyer for the underclass of Berlin and editor of the *Police Journal*; in his spare time he was a paid police *agent provocateur*, sniffing out radicals and anti-monarchists. In 1848 Stieber, quite by chance, saved the life of Frederic Wilhelm IV,

King of Prussia, when the sovereign was surrounded by a hostile mob. Until his descent into insanity in 1857, Frederick Wilhelm showered preferment on Stieber who became Commissioner of Police in 1850. However, Stieber lost favour during the regency of Frederic Wilhelm's brother (later Kaiser Wilhelm I) and decamped to St Petersburg where he put to good use his knowledge of Russian revolutionaries; those he had monitored included the German socialist in exile Karl Marx in the London of the 1850s. Stieber advised, too, on the establishment of an external spy system for Russia within the Secret Police Department of State Protection of Czar Alexander II, which ultimately became the *Okhrannoye Otdyelyenye* (OKHRANA).

By 1863 Stieber was back in Germany and won an introduction to the Prusso-German Prince Otto Leopold von Bismarck, then busy with his plans for the ascendancy of Prussia on the European political scene. Stieber advanced state espionage in the Seven Weeks' War against Austria (1863) and founded a new section of the secret police (with himself as commander) which was to survive within the *Geheimefeldpolizei* (Secret Field Police) of the Second World War. Through his innovations Stieber almost invented counter-espionage, and this aspect, with its use of military censorship and false propaganda, appealed to the Japanese, trawling as they were for a mentor for their own embryonic secret service.

After his successful ground work of agent infiltration during the Franco-Prussian War 1870–1, Stieber began to organise a network of permanent resident spies abroad which the Japanese were to ape in China. And as Minister of Police, Stieber was to introduce another of his innovations monitored by the Japanese and later used by the Kempeitai. It took the form of a brothel pandering to sexual aberrations. To it came a clientele of the high ranking who could be pumped for information while in passionate pursuit, and their perversions later exploited with a little blackmail. It was to be the jewel in Stieber's intelligence

23

network. The Japanese set up a similar house at Hankow (Wuhan, capital of Hubei Province) called the 'Hall of Pleasurable Delights'. It offered a cornucopia of oriental perversion for decadent Chinese leaders, but it served a second function as a meeting place for Japanese agents operating in Sinkiang (modern Xinjiang Uygur Autonomous Region, North-West China) and Russian-governed Central Asia.

All of his ideas, then, Wilhelm Stieber sold to the Japanese who incorporated them into their own espionage system, with modifications to suit the oriental theatre of operations. They further strengthened their spy service using an area of expertise they already had. Throughout Japan there was a network of *himitsu kessha* (secret societies) fired with *aikokushin* (patriotic nationalism). One such was the *Genyosha* ('Black Ocean Society'). Founded as *Kayosha* (national assembly pressure group) by Mitsura Toyama with Kotaro Hiraoka and Rokusuke Hakoda, the society was renamed, in the year of the Kempeitai's birth (1881), after the strip of water called the *genkai nada* which separates Kyushu from mainland Korea. The society agitated for Japan to play a greater role in Asian affairs and advocated Japanese expansionism on the Chinese continent. Toyama's tenets were the breath of life for Japan's military cadre and for proponents of Kempeitai goals.

The *Genyosha* became the precursor of a whole range of patriotic societies all working for the discovery and manipulation of the weaknesses of China and Russia. Propaganda societies were spawned, too, like the *Dai-A-Gi Kai* ('Re-awakening of Greater Asia' Society) to promote Sino-Japanese *rapprochement*. In Shanghai the Tung Wen College was founded to train Japanese agents in East Asia. By 1908 it was sending graduates from Burma to the Philippines and was supported by the Kempeitai, by 1937, in buildings of Chiaotung University. Known colloquially as the 'Japanese Spy College' by the Chinese, it functioned until Japanese capitulation in 1945. All of these, and the foreign language schools set up by the Japanese, were to be used for their own ends by the Kempeitai.

The *Sambo Hombu* was established in 1878 and led to the formation of the *Joho-kikan* (Army Intelligence Service). Army intelligence was a function of the 2nd Bureau of the *Sambo Hombu*, comprising the 5th Section (the US, Canada, South America and Europe), 6th Section (Asiatic) and a Secret Section (general secret service) headed by a *shosho*. Intelligence officers were assigned to army, division and regimental staffs. The Kempeitai had most contact with the *Tokumu Kikan* (Special Service Agency) of military intelligence which was directly under the orders of the *Daihonei* (Imperial General HQ); this gave them an essential by-passing of the complicated organisation of general intelligence of the High Command. Thus the *Tokumu Kikan* had a joint interest with the Kempeitai in espionage, counter-espionage, propaganda and fifth-column activities, as did the *Hikari Kikan*, a parallel civil intelligence and sabotage organisation.

It was the Kempeitai, however, who used the supposed threat of enemy espionage as a political tool. When the Japanese Diet passed a new anti-espionage law in 1939, the Kempeitai were given much wider opportunities for manipulation of the death penalty. They set up exhibitions of 'enemy espionage' techniques and supposed equipment to heighten public awareness of the inherent dangers of fraternisation with any foreign nationals, and they promoted 'Anti-Spy-Days' to encourage ordinary folk to be vigilant at all times against enemy agents. There was not a single shop in Japan that did not display a Kempeitai propaganda poster on one subject or another.

III Political Influence

Because of *Taisho* (general; and later *Sori-daijin*) Hideki Tojo's involvement with the Kempeitai in the early days of his military career the Military Police always had a great influence in and on Japanese politics throughout the 1930s. This influence was enhanced by the power structure of the military cadres in Japanese government. During March 1936 the cabinet of the naval leader and statesman *Sori-daijin* Keisuke Okada fell due to heavy pressure on him from the military and rural-bourgeoise political party known as the *Seiyukai*. His residence was even attacked by young army officers, but he escaped assassination. Okada's position was taken by Koki Hirota, but because of military influence the appointments to his new cabinet had to be approved by the *Rikugun-daijin Taisho* Hisaichi Terauchi.

Japan steadily fell into anti-democratic rule, taking such steps as the signing of the Anti-Comintern Pact of December 1936 with the National Socialist Germany of Adolf Hitler. Internal strife within government finally brought the fall of Hirota. The emperor requested *Taisho* Kozushige Ugaki to form a government. On his way to the *Kyujo* to meet the emperor, Ugaki's car was stopped by *Chujo* (Lt-Gen.) Kisayo Nakajima, head of the Kempeitai. Ugaki was informed that the Army (and the Kempeitai) would not accept him as *Sori-daijin*. In the event the position was given to 'All-things-to-all-men' *Koshaku* (Prince) Fumimaro Konoye.

The military grip on Japan tightened and Konoye talked of the *Toa Shinchitsujo* (New Order of Asia) which expressed the philosophy of Japanese hegemony in the Orient; the *Kokumin Seishi Sodoin Undo* (National Spiritual Mobilisation Movement) was instituted, too, to lead and control thinking in Japanese policy-making. And Kempeitai powers were extended. To round off the increased military control it was announced that the new *Jikan Rikugun-daijin* was the 'old Kempeitai-hand' Hideki Tojo. Kempeitai personnel now became super-active throughout Japan and there was no commercial, government or private door closed to them.

26

IV *Tokei-Tai – The Naval Secret Police*

The inherent rivalry between the *Dai Nippon Teikoku Rikugun* and the *Dai Nippon Teikoku Kaigun* encouraged the latter to resist the excesses of the Kempeitai with respect to naval employees and personnel. And from pre-1946 documents it can be seen that the *Kaigun-daijin* issued instructions limiting their control. In any case the Navy had its own Naval Secret Police, the no less loathed (in the Occupied Territories) *Tokei-tai*.

In the history of the Second World War in the Far East the *Tokei-tai* have a much lower profile than the Kempeitai. But during the period October 1943 to June 1944, the *Tokei-tai* were to earn infamy in what had been Dutch colonial Borneo. Here the *Tokei-tai* were concerned to crush any anti-Japanese resistance movements.

Throughout the Naval Control Area – for which after 1943 the *Dai Nippon Teikoku Kaigun* had their own overprinted postage stamps – these *Tokei-tai* kept up the myth that they were continually suppressing these 'resistance movements'. They supported the myth with a huge number of 'confessions' extracted under torture; following one farcical 'spy trial', they executed sixty-three innocent Chinese, Dutch and Indonesian civilians.

The *Tokei-tai* carried out a programme of mass murder. It is estimated that they slaughtered a thousand people at Mandor by the direct orders of the *Dai Nippon Teikoku Kaigun* headquarters at Sourabaya. The reports of *Tokei-tai Tai-i* (Military Police Naval Lieutenant) Yamamoto confirm that another 240 were killed at Sunggei Durian; and countless hundreds at Katapang and the port of Pontianak. Among prominent victims were the Sultan of Pontianak and his two sons.

During August 1944, the *Tokei-tai* were active in the repression and execution of 120 Chinese civilians at Singkawang, Western Borneo, mostly without trial. In his famous study of Japanese War Crimes, *The Knights of the Bushido* (1958), Lord Russell of

Liverpool quotes a *Tokei-tai Tsuyaku* (Military Naval Police interpreter) called Hayashi who left this report of the Singkawang massacres:

> In August 1944 I discovered that some Chinese were holding a meeting in Singkawang. I reported this to my superior Okajima, who gave me a list of fifty people to arrest. After arresting them I interrogated them. After the electric and water treatments had been applied they admitted conspiring to overthrow the Japanese Military Government. I took part in the torturing. In my opinion all these hundred and twenty people had committed no crime and had been involved in no conspiracy. They were arrested on account of their wealth. The whole affair was a plot executed by three members of the *Tokei-tai* and myself. The confessions purporting to have been made by the suspects during interrogation were, in reality, drawn up by the *Tokei-tai* beforehand, and were only signed by their supposed authors after torture. We anticipated that the death sentence would be given on the strength of these reports. They were most wealthy and important people and it was, therefore, better to kill them. Their money and valuables were confiscated by the *Tokei-tai*.

The *Tokei-tai* operated in areas in which the Kempeitai had a large presence too. For instance, a *Tokei-tai* unit occupied the St Andrews Mission Hospital, Singapore.

V The Kempeitai Vis-à-Vis the Gestapo

Several writers on Second World War matters, from the authors of PoW memoirs to military historians, have compared the Kempeitai with the *Geheimstaatspolizei* (Secret State Police) of Hitler's National Socialist Germany. The latter force had evolved from a small department of the Prussian State Police, under its chief Hermann

Wilhelm Göring, to become the tangled bureaucracy of state terror dubbed the Gestapo.

It is a felicitous enough and easily understood comparison, but the inferences that the Kempeitai owed anything to the Gestapo, or had reciprocal agreements or a policy of cooperation with it are misleading. The Japanese military and naval commands were acquainted with *Nationalsozialistische Deutsche Arbeiterpartei* (National Socialist German Workers' Party) propaganda and Gestapo techniques, yet they did not specifically follow National Socialist philosophy or practices, and never had an equivalent of Reinhard Heydrich's *Einsatzgruppen* (SS Special Action Groups) extermination squads. Nor was there ever a figure in Kempeitai lore like Heinrich Himmler, who moulded the Gestapo into a 'cleanser' of political, racial and homosexual 'deviants' motivated solely by a drive towards a race of pure supermen. The Kempeitai were bent on reducing any opposition to the concept of *Hakko Ichiu*. Thus, too, the role and character of the Kempeitai were never shaped by the personal ambitions of its individual leaders as in the Gestapo. It may be added, though, that there were some parallels between the *Waffen SS*, particularly the *Totenkopfverbände* (Death's Head Divisions), when the Kempeitai acted as camp guardians in occupied South East Asia.

When Japan withdrew from the League of Nations, Hitler's National Socialists developed a greater interest in the country; an interest that had begun in Germany in the 1920s. The National Socialist Party speculated that Japan would go to war with Russia over imperialist possessions in Asia. Hitler even had conversations with *Shosho* Hiroshi Oshima (1936; *Chujo* and *Taishi* – 'ambassador' – to Germany, 1938), military attaché to Berlin who was known to be pro-German.

Oshima also had known links with Admiral Wilhelm Canaris, head of the German *Abwehr* (Military Intelligence), which played a prominent role in German espionage and counter-espionage, the very remit of the Kempeitai; but this did not lead to cooperation. In fact, both the Gestapo and the Kempeitai were wary of each other. The National Socialist Party agents and the Kempeitai both, yet separately, monitored all German Embassy staff and businessmen in Japan. The German RSHA (*Reichssicherheitshauptamt* – Reich Central Security Office) had seven services (*Amter*); AMT VI – Police Intelligence (External) had a division called the VIC; this department surveyed Japan.

The first National Socialist Party groups were organised in Japan in Tokyo and Yokohama in the mid-months of 1934, under the leadership of *Landesgruppenleiter* Rudolf Hillmann. There were around 200 such members in Japan and their work was mainly to promote anti-semitism and anti-communist propaganda, and to monitor the Japanese agreement to the Anti-Comintern Pact negotiated by *Shosho* Oshima. The Japanese in general disliked the National Socialist members' arrogance and contempt for the Japanese, and the Kempeitai kept a permanent tail on the German Ambassador to Japan, General Eugene Ott, and the German military attaché at Tokyo, General Kretschmer. They also monitored the activities of the 'police attachés' appointed to German embassies and consulates which operated under orders from Heinrich Himmler and the Head of the Department of Germans Abroad, Ernst Wilhelm Bohle.

There is a little evidence that Gestapo officers did assist the Japanese civil police. One such instance is quoted by John Morris, who in 1938 was employed as an adviser and university lecturer by the *Gaimusho*. In his *Traveller from Tokyo* (1943), Morris noted that Gestapo Colonel Meisinger 'had been sent to Japan to give the police the benefit of his experience'. This visit in itself is not surprising for Japan had espoused Prussian advice on reorganising the Army, and Major Jacob Meckel taught the art of war at the Japanese War College.

The Japanese secret services, including the Kempeitai, maintained a watching brief in Germany through the Manchuquo

Embassy and the Japanese Embassy, and through *Taisho* Komatsu. Secret dossiers from Europe were coordinated by *Taishi* Onodera at Stockholm. The Japanese, through the Kempeitai, actively helped the Polish Resistance Movement. As the head of SS Foreign Intelligence, Walter Schellenberg, noted in his *Memoirs* (1956): 'Poland was an especially interesting field for [the Japanese] as it could be used for intelligence work in two directions, against the Germans and against the Russians.'

CHAPTER TWO

KEMPEITAI RECRUITMENT, DISTRIBUTION AND DUTIES

The nations of the world are committing a most terrible mistake in dealing with the Japanese as though they were a civilized people. It is a grievous error, and one likely to prove catastrophic in its consequences.

Amleto Vespa, Italian diplomat, Manchuria, 1938

I   Enlisted Personnel

By the time western intelligence was preparing its dossiers on Japanese secret police and espionage in the late 1930s they were able to see that the Kempeitai were made up of *sakan* (field officers), *kashikan* (non-commissioned officers) and *jotohei* (superior privates). When needed, *ittohei* (first class privates) and *nitohei* (second class privates) were attached from other services. Officers were recruited from other branches of the *Dai Nippon Teikoku Rikugun* on permanent assignment to the Kempeitai, and in peacetime these officers were volunteers from the ranks of those of 'good character' and 'high physical standard'. In wartime officers were drawn from all service branches, as needed.

Officers and enlisted men underwent training either in military police schools or special training units, as well as attending courses in Kempeitai theory and practice at unit barracks. The main Kempeitai schools were at Tokyo and Keijo (modern Seoul), Korea; during the war there were also schools at Singapore and Manila.

From 1881, Kempeitai officers were usually graduates of the *Rikugun Shikan Gakko* (Military Academy, leading on from the *Rikugun Yasen Gakko*, military preparatory schools), or the *Rikugun Daigako* (General Staff College). Six years of commissioned rank training was the norm, while in wartime training as Kempeitai lasted one year on an ad hoc basis; in peacetime NCO courses lasted six months. Kempeitai personnel were of higher educational standard and of better physique than the ordinary soldier. In 1938 the *Koho Kimmu Yoin Yoseijo* (Rear Service Personnel Training Centre) was opened at Kudan, Tokyo, under *Chujo* Eiichi Kinoshita, where Kempeitai officers received secret intelligence instruction. Training included espionage, use of explosives, fifth-column organisation, code breaking, effective burglary and horsemanship. Foreign language study was low-key and in the field the Kempeitai usually employed (often inadequate) interpreters. Courses in disguise were held too, and trainees were sent incognito to companies to make reports while remaining undetected. In wartime Kempeitai officers were recruited for training from the *Gaimusho* and diplomatic staffs.

Kempeitai officers were referred to as *Kempeitai Taisa* (Military Police Colonel) or *Kempeitai Tai-i* (Military Police Captain), and so on. For normal duties the Kempeitai wore the uniform of the *Kihei Rentai* (cavalry regiment) with heavy boots of undressed black leather. A cavalry sabre and regulation revolver were carried by officers, while other ranks sported bayonet and pistol. Officers' sidearms were the *Nambu* 8 mm pistol of 1925–39 vintage (in a leather holster with belt loops and shoulder straps) and the Meiji 30 rifle. A white armband with the two calligraphic characters for Kempeitai (*Ken* − 'law' *hei* − 'soldier') was worn on the left arm, while the upper arm insignia was the elongated 'M' of the army with black central colouring. Sometimes the calligraphy was red on khaki. During the Second World War the Allies were used to the Kempeitai wearing the M1938 khaki field dress for officers, NCOs and enlisted men. Plain clothes were also worn when relevant, but some Kempeitai functionaries wore badges of the correct insignia, or the imperial chrysanthemum on the underside of jacket lapels.

Writing in 1945 of Japan in the years before the First World War, the teacher-missionary Phyllis Argall remembered the 'plummage' of earlier Kempeitai:

There were another group of men in Okayama [then a country town in western Honshu] who occasionally rode horseback. They wore green coats, black trousers with yellow stripes down the sides, high black boots and caps banded in red. I asked my father once what they were. He told me they were gendarmes [the term was erroneous]. I asked what 'gendarmes' meant. He explained that it was a French word for military police. Even that was not very clear to me, nor did I find out exactly what their duties were. I did gather, however, that they were to be feared with the fear awarded to the police force and the army combined. Twenty-five years later my childhood question was answered, and I received a liberal education in the ways, duties, and methods of the gendarmes, though, by 1941 they had discarded their brilliant plummage. [Argall became a PoW in 1941.]

Some lower-ranking Kempeitai (i.e. *gocho*, corporals) − as PoWs were to note painfully − carried bamboo swords usually used in the traditional Japanese sword-handling sports such as *Kendo*. Herein the bamboo was split to make it more pliable and it could inflict painful, stinging blows.

As Japanese militarism and imperialism began to escalate in the 1930s, western powers assessed that there were 315 Kempeitai officers serving in 1937 and 6,000 other ranks. By the beginning of the Second World War the number of officers had increased to 601 regular officers allocated thus, as set out by the US *Handbook of Japanese Military Forces* (1942):

Japan and Karafuto, 142; Manchuria, 114; Korea 23; Formosa 24; North China, 100; Central China, 97; South China, 16; and, the Southern Area (including Field Units) 85.

Records examined after the Second World War gave the following figures for Kempeitai strength at the height of hostilities.

Japan, 10,679   Kwangtung Army, 4,946
Korea, 1,927   Central China, 6,115
North China, 4,253   French Indochina, 479
South China, 1,094   Malaya, 758
Singapore, 362   Burma, 540
Thailand, 937   Sumatra, 387
Philippines, 829   Borneo, 156
Java, 538   South Seas, 89
Formosa, 745

The 1942 *Handbook*, quoting a report from China and dated March 1940, noted that the 'basic military–police unit' was made up of forty men under a *Tai-i* or *Chu-i*. It is likely that unit size varied as to war theatre necessity and that Kempeitai detachments varied in size and composition according to the area of service and duties undertaken.

The structure of Kempeitai command may be summarised thus:

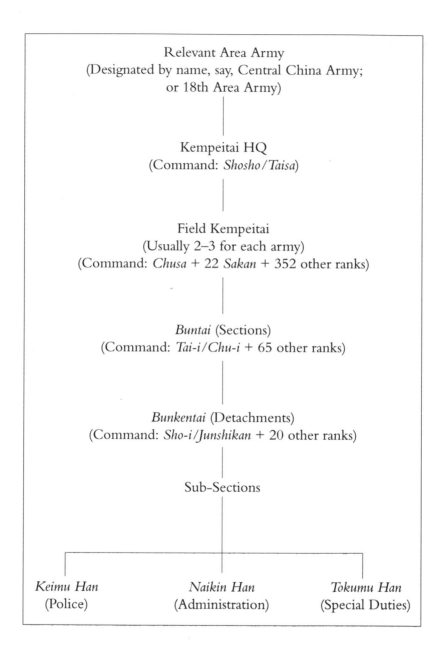

Relevant Area Army
(Designated by name, say, Central China Army;
or 18th Area Army)

Kempeitai HQ
(Command: *Shosho/Taisa*)

Field Kempeitai
(Usually 2–3 for each army)
(Command: *Chusa* + 22 *Sakan* + 352 other ranks)

Buntai (Sections)
(Command: *Tai-i/Chu-i* + 65 other ranks)

Bunkentai (Detachments)
(Command: *Sho-i/Junshikan* + 20 other ranks)

Sub-Sections

| *Keimu Han* | *Naikin Han* | *Tokumu Han* |
| (Police) | (Administration) | (Special Duties) |

Because Kempeitai personnel largely 'went underground' after the Japanese surrender, and many records were deliberately destroyed by both the Japanese authorities and the Occupation Forces, it has been a difficult task for western historians to identify prominent Kamikaze officers. The following Kempeitai may be mentioned as being representative as career officers of the highest ranks.

Shosho Hirano Toyoji.   Commander of the Kempeitai unit of the 25th Army; arrived at Padang, West Sumatra by 1944

Taisho Rokuro Iwasa.   Commander-in-Chief Kempeitai HQ, Tokyo around 1936

Shosho Hokujiro Kato.   Held concurrent positions as Commander of North China Expeditionary Force Kempeitai and Commander of the Special Garrison Unit at Beijing and Hopeh Province

Shosho Eiichi Kinoshita.   Commander Eastern District Kempeitai, 1945. Arrested by US Occupying Forces as suspected war criminal.

Shosho Kenzo Kitano.   Prominent officer with background in military training and inspectorate; served in German Embassy, Berlin, 1922; chief of Kempeitai in China, 1939.

Shosho Kenshichi Masuoka.   Commander of Kempeitai in the Philippines. Arrested as war criminal, sentenced to ten years hard labour at Manila.

Shosho Takeshi Mori.   Prominent cavalry and General Staff Officer. Deputy-chief Kempeitai, 1943. Assassinated in 1945 *coup*

of rebel army officers who attempted to continue the war and prevent surrender.

Chujo Sanji Okido.   Prominent General Staff Officer. Commander of the Kempeitai, HQ Kudan, Tokyo 1944–5.

Taisho Shinokura.   Identified as Commander of all Kempeitai forces in Japan and Occupied Territories by 1945. Committed suicide, 1945.

Chujo Makoto Tsukomoto.   Commander Formosa Kempeitai by 1945.

II *Distribution*
Regional Organisation

Under the command of *Homengun shireibu* (Army Area HQ) within Japan proper or base areas in main puppet/occupied countries.

a Japanese homeland and the Karafuto Arc

During peacetime the home-based Kempeitai were organised (by the 1930s) within the four Army Areas (developed from the old pre–1914 Army Corps Presidencies) into units corresponding to the fourteen divisional districts with individual headquarters at the relevant depot divisions.

In wartime the Kempeitai districts were allocated by the *Rikugun-daijin* taking into consideration the needs of the local population and industrial/munitions complexes. By way of example: the port of Kobe, the prefectural capital of Hyogo on Osaka Bay, at the entrance to the *Seto Naikai* (Inland Sea), was a strategic port of the Hanshin industrial belt. This came within the Himeji City divisional area assigned to the Osaka Kempeitai. As

Kobe possessed an important naval dockyard (of the Kawasaki Shipbuilding Co.) there was a strong naval presence which led to the usual Army/Navy rivalry. As the need for top security developed the units were formed at places like the naval bases of Kure (which had an important naval arsenal) and Yokosuka (with its ordnance depot).

A regional organisation of the Kempeitai was based north of the main island of Hokkaido for the Karafuto Arc of the Kurile Islands. This area had been recognised as Japanese territory by the Czarist government in 1875.

b Korea, Formosa and Manchuria/Manchuquo

All the main towns of Korea and Formosa had detachments of Kempeitai. Both were commanded by *Shosho*, whereas a *Chujo* commanded the Kwangtung (Guangdong, South China) Kempeitai from a headquarters at Xinjing (modern Changchun), the Japanese-controlled capital of puppet Manchuquo. From here all the areas of Manchuria were overseen by the Kempeitai.

c China and the Southern Area

The Kempeitai were under a *Shosho* in Northern and Central China, while in Southern China a *Taisa* was the most senior officer. By 1942 the Southern Expeditionary Force Kempeitai Training Unit had established themselves at Singapore (*Synonan* to the Japanese), and Kempeitai activity in this area was under the command of field Kempeitai units.

Yasen Kempeitai

These were numbered field units, operating in forward/fighting areas. Various headquarters were up set for these field units. For example, the port and capital of East New Britain at Rabaul, New

Guinea, was singled out for such a command base for operations in the areas of the Solomon Islands and the Bismarck Archipelago; at the zenith of its powers in August 1942, this was the south-eastern limit of the *Dai Nippon Teikoku*.

Kempeitai Auxiliaries

Recruitment of volunteer ethnic auxiliaries of the Kempeitai was established by the laws of 1919 and 1937, such volunteers to work in subject Korea and Manchuquo. They were only allowed to reach the rank of *shocho* (Sgt-major) and came under the command of the Kempeitai units of the area in which they were to operate.

III Duties

In Japan's war theatres the Kempeitai issued travel permits, recruited labour, winkled out and arrested fifth-columnists, requisitioned food and supplies, started propaganda programmes and scotched subversive anti-Japanese rumours. Any members of the Kempeitai had the power to arrest personnel up to three ranks higher than themselves.

In occupied countries the Kempeitai were to organise ethnic help groups. In the area from Attu and Kiska Islands (in the Aleutians) in the north, to the Marshall and Gilbert Islands in the south (to the west of the International Date Line), the Kempeitai were mandated to 'pacifying hostile natives', and to 'settle disputes between the natives and Japanese soldiers', notes the US *Handbook of Japanese Military Forces*. This included the organisation of native spy networks for operation in occupied zones and behind enemy lines. A captured Japanese report noted how in New Guinea native peoples were recruited for reconnaissance work and to form groups 'to harass the enemy'. Another such order to the Kempeitai commander at Lae (Papua New Guinea, on Huan

Gulf) directed him to 'complete the training of the native "army"'.

PoW Camp Surveillance

PoW camps (*furyu shuyojo*) were run by the *Naimusho* until 7 November 1943, thereafter by the *Rikugunsho*. The Kempeitai monitored the activities and had governance over all *furyo* (PoWs), and searched and screened all bound for camps in Japan.

Camp duties were usually undertaken by Kempeitai *kashikan* bent on discovering stealable goods, radios and diaries. Men from one group at Tamaran camp, near Kanchanburie, Thailand, and bound for Japan had several such diaries. Private Roy H. Whitecross of the 8th Division of the Australian Army (AIF) remembered this incident in his *Slaves of the Son of Heaven* (1952). It was an event that was repeated hundreds of times in the course of PoW history:

> I dashed down to Maurice's [Pte Maurice Alan Barklay] hut. 'The [Kempeitai] are searching the fellows' gear at the gate!' I cried. 'What about our diaries?'
>
> 'We'll have to entrust them to someone remaining in the camp,' he said. 'It would be suicide to try and take them with us.'
>
> 'How would it be if I got someone to seal them in a tin and bury them in camp. They could be dug up after the war, either by us or someone else.'
>
> The project was discussed with Eric Hirsch, a friend of mine from Div. H.Q., who was working in a small tool shed built near the camp well. At my suggestion Eric agreed to find two tins. Our papers were to be sealed into the small one, which would be placed inside the larger one. He promised to bury them under the floor of the tool shed, which was exactly thirty-seven paces south of the well. This well we considered to be the most permanent landmark in the camp. These arrangements were

carried out, and eighteen months later the papers were dug up by Eric Hirsch and taken home.

The Kempeitai were often involved in rooting out pilfering in prison camps. A.G. Allbury, gunner with the 18th Division, when at Havelock Road PoW Camp, Singapore recalled an incident when four men were caught by the Kempeitai having stolen rice when on dock duty. He left this memory in his *Bamboo and Bushido* (1955):

> The [Kempeitai] started searching us from each end of the column simultaneously. There were grunts and gasps of pain as they discovered the first culprits. Bottles and bags were hastily passed from hand to hand and seized by those in the back row. Those with rice in their pockets stealthily changed positions. Water running in the malarial drain behind us began to flow white as the rice was emptied into it. By the time the Japs had searched half of the front row there was nothing left on us to be found.
>   But they caught four men.
>   They dragged them out of the ranks and gave them the most savagely brutal beating–up. Sweating and grunting, their vicious yellow faces distorted with rage, they continued to thud heavy boots into the prostrate figures on the ground long after the men had lost consciousness. The dockside, still smiling in the warm evening sun, became suddenly a terrible place to be in.

And as Jim Ford CB MC of the Royal Scots remembered from the time when he was a PoW in a Japanese mainland camp: 'I noticed that the Kempeitai were feared as much by the Japanese as by the prisoners. Although of comparatively junior rank they walked into camps or workplaces without hindrance and shouted orders at officers and civilians alike. They were swaggering bullies and used physical attack as a matter of course.'

Reprisal Duty

The Kempeitai organised regular reprisals against rebellious native populations. In September 1944, such retribution was ordered by the old-Kempeitai hand *Taisho* Shizuichi Tanaka in the Timor (Lesser Sundas, Indonesia) theatre. The Kempeitai had long been active against the natives at Loeang and Sermata Islands, and a number of Kempeitai had been assassinated. Tanaka ordered a wave of interrogation, torture and punishment and the Rajah of Loeang was ordered to root out the assassins. He failed and was executed along with ninety-six islanders.

June 1945 saw the position of the Japanese forces in Burma turn precarious. For some time British paratroopers had been teaming up with local guerrillas to harry Japanese positions at Tenasserim, between Moulmein (the city-port capital of Mon state) and Dali Forest. *Shosho* Seiei Yamamoto, Chief of Staff to the 33rd Army under *Chujo* Masaki Hondo ordered a group of soldiers from the 3rd Battalion the 215th Regiment and OC Moulmein Kempeitai to sweep Kalagon and kill as many British paratroopers and *dacoits* (Burmese bandits) as possible. By 7 July they had occupied the village and all the inhabitants were rounded up to be interrogated by the Kempeitai. Although women and children were raped and beaten, no information about the resistance movement was elicited and the Kempeitai ordered the whole village to be massacred. The people were taken tied up, in batches of five to ten, to a nearby group of wells. There they were blindfolded and bayoneted into the wells, alive or not. On that day the 3rd Battalion and the Kempeitai killed 600 villagers.

IV *Women, Prostitution and the Kempeitai*

Women were used as informers by the Kempeitai in reasonably large numbers in the occupied countries, because of their role in domestic service. Few women were ever recorded as serving in the ranks of the Kempeitai. One exception was Madam Nogami, a prominent member of the International Settlement of occupied Shanghai. She was nicknamed 'Queen Cobra' by the foreign residents, and was active before and after the Settlement was taken by Commander-in-Chief of Central China Area Army, *Taisho* Iwane Matsui ('The Butcher of Nanking'). According to the German correspondent and agent Captain Walter Steenes, Nogami rose to the rank of *Kempeitai Tai-i*. It is reported that she committed suicide on the Japanese surrender.

When Korea (1904) and Manchuria (1931) came under Japanese occupation, the Kempeitai controlled the new system of prostitution management in these areas. They supervised registration of prostitutes, provided medical checks and reported instances of sexually transmitted disease. In recent years research work has been done on the officially registered brothels set up during the Second World War by the Imperial Japanese Forces throughout the occupied Far East. Chinese, Korean, Indonesian, Malay and Filipino women and girls were enslaved and forced into prostitution to service the Japanese Army and Navy. Their plight has been until lately one of the lesser-known horror stories of the Second World War.

The Kempeitai were key administrators in the general organisation of these *jugun ianfu* ('comfort women'). Women were either duped into prostitution or abducted for sexual purposes by collaborators (including civil police) within their own ethnic groups. Kempeitai arrested women who were reluctant. Eurasians were in great demand for sex at Japanese officers' clubs, and white women from PoW camps were pressurised into prostitution through deliberate starvation and having to suffer poor living quarters. Dutch women from Dutch Indonesia and captured Australian nurses were particularly vulnerable. Some civilian women did collaborate in providing sex in return for food, cigarettes, medicines and the safety of their children.

Jugun ianfu were transported to the front by the Japanese Army

The Kempeitai introduced cage brothels in Occupied Territories as part of the systematic debauching of the native population. During the Second World War the Kempeitai were active in coercing women in Korea and South East Asia into prostitution to act as 'comfort women' for Japanese troops. (JRP)

and Navy transport systems, and some were flown into war theatres. In January 1942 the *Gaimu-daijin* Shigenori Togo ordered that the comfort women be issued with military travel papers. The *karayuki* (Japanese travelling prostitutes) usually served high-ranking Japanese officers.

The Kempeitai also controlled violence and drunkenness at brothels, regulated accommodation and checked identity. This deposition was left by a Kempeitai soldier on this matter: 'The

Kempeitai kept an accurate account of the number of times a soldier visited a *ianjo* [comfort house]. Given the low rate of pay of the soldiers [Kempeitai] suspicions would be raised if a rank and file soldier visited such a house more than once or twice a month. . . . Too great a frequency might indicate that a soldier was trafficking in a prohibited substance or was defrauding the local populace.'

The Kempeitai used women as agents at broadcasting stations. The Japanese Broadcasting Corporation (NHK – *Nihon Hoso Kyokai*) was supervised by the Electrical Affairs Bureau of the *Teishinsho* (Communications Ministry). NHK controlled the country's central short-wave station Radio Tokyo, and there were also wartime satellite stations at Batavia, Saigon, Shanghai and Singapore. Overseas broadcasting was slowly increased at the outbreak of war, and after the devastating defeat at the Battle of Midway (June 1942), the Overseas Bureau was expanded to include broadcasts to the US, Europe and Asia (including Oceania) with re-vamped editorial departments. Although the Kempeitai had agents throughout the broadcasting network, they were particularly active in the field of broadcasting to the 'front line' and areas where there were PoW establishments (the latter came under the department responsible for handling US matters.).

One of the most famous propaganda programmes was *Zero Hour* which told indigenous peoples that they would be tortured and killed by US personnel if captured. Many broadcasts were aimed at women abroad, inciting them to help stop the war. The radio stations used a large number of *Nisei* (persons born in the US of Japanese parentage) and enemy nationals. PoWs were forced to broadcast propaganda; yet non-Japanese accented broadcasters peddling such lines as 'The Nipponese people don't want to fight . . . they want to be friends', held little credibility in occupied countries. *Zero Hour* was to make several Japanese female broadcasters famous, like Fumo Saisho from the Shanghai station, and many a Kempeitai recruit won celebrity over the airwaves as 'Tokyo Rose'.

'Tokyo Rose' was the nickname given by US military and naval personnel to a group of English-speaking female broadcasters on Radio Tokyo short-wave programmes. The term was generally used after 1943. GIs were to build the myth of 'Tokyo Rose' into a sinister, seductive-voiced Japanese broadcaster who lured the US military to death and surrender, while taunting them with sadistic propaganda. Yet the voice and the patriotic march *Aikoku koshin kyoku* played before each broadcast made for compulsive listening. It was the theme song of Radio Tokyo and was a useful 'test' to tune in to. Its verses included words of pure Kempeitai bluff:

Yuke, hakko ieto nashi   Onward, east, west, north and south,
         Over land and main.

Shikaino hito michibikite   Let us make the world our home
         Call to fellow men.

Tadashiki heiwa uchitaten   Everywhere on the four seas
         Let us build the tower

Risawa hanato sakikaoru   of just peace – let our ideal
         Bloom forth like a flower.

The soubriquet of 'Tokyo Rose' was to be particularly associated with Iva Toguri Di Aquino, a *nisei* stranded by war in Japan. She was born at Los Angeles, California, on 4 July 1912 to Jun and Fumi Toguri and graduated from the University of California. She travelled to Japan in July 1941 to see a sick aunt. On the outbreak of war she was interrogated by the *Tokko keisatsu*. Her file was passed to the Kempeitai who pressed her to renounce her US citizenship and become a Japanese. She refused.

For a while she worked as a private music teacher and went on

47

Iva Toguri earned the name 'Tokyo Rose' for her 'sweet music and sour propaganda' on NHK's Zero Hour programme to Allied troops. The Kempeitai regularly targeted Japanese-Americans like Toguri to work on propaganda projects and as interrogators. (Hulton Getty Picture Collection)

to become a radio monitor for *Domei* (Japanese News Agency). She continued to be harassed by the TOKKO and the Kempeitai concerning her citizenship. This harassment and her need to earn a living led her to apply for a secretarial post at Radio Tokyo. Soon she was to appear on *Zero Hour* as a propaganda broadcaster under the guidance of *Shosho* Shigetsugu Tsuneishi who specialised in forcing PoWs to broadcast.

She continued this work until the end of the war. Iva Toguri was arrested by US Counter Intelligence Officers from Yokohama on 17 October 1945 and taken to Sugamo prison. There she remained for a year suspected of being a Kempeitai stooge; she was released without prosecution. Iva Toguri was to be caught up in the growing US public demand to 'move in on a number of World War II treason cases'. Re-arrested on 26 August 1948, she was charged with 'treasonable conduct against the United States Government during World War II', and transferred to San Francisco. Her trial commenced on 5 July 1949 at the Federal District Court, San Francisco, Northern District of California. Eight counts were brought against her, but she was found guilty of only one (broadcasting on the outcome of the Leyte Gulf action of October 1944). She served a prison sentence until 1956. Many believed that she was put on trial for political reasons; so many Kempeitai officers, for instance, had escaped retribution that revenge was sought at the highest level. Iva Toguri was given an unconditional pardon by President Gerald Ford on 19 January 1977.

It is curious to note that rumours spread in the USA that the Kempeitai had recruited flyer Amelia Earhart to broadcast as 'Tokyo Rose'. She had disappeared in mid-flight over the Pacific in July 1937 and reports picked up by US radio monitors stated that a women with an American accent was broadcasting for the Japanese. (Many of the *nisei* had American accents.) The US government even flew out Earhart's husband George Palmer Putnam to the Pacific theatre to listen to the voice. His denials that the voice was that of his wife did nothing to stem the rumours.

V   Bacterial Warfare and Medical Experiments

The Japanese did not use gas warfare in the Second World War, but incorporated anti-gas measures into army training. The Kempeitai were involved in collecting victims on which to experiment with gas. Yet this was only one aspect of gathering the damned for medical experimentation. Kempeitai prisoners who were recalcitrant were sent to 'human experiment' units. Thus some 3,000 Chinese, Russians, Koreans, Europeans and Americans alone were sent to the notorious 150-building compound of Unit 731. The Army set up this unit in 1932 in the Beiyinhe district of Harbin, Manchuquo, as an extension of the biological and chemical warfare centre pioneered by Emperor Hirohito's father-in-law *Chujo* Prince Kuniyoshi Kuni in the late 1920s. At Unit 731 vivisection and artificially induced disease, frostbite and horrific simulated war wounds were all part of the experiments carried out on human beings. The Kempeitai organised a Human Materials Procurement Arm for this work and the laboratories were moved to Pingfang (*Heibo* to the Japanese) in 1936. Unit 731 was supplied with *maruta* ('logs', Kempeitai jargon for prisoners) ferried in windowless prison cars along the China-Manchuria Railway. Some were brought via the nearby airfield which dispatched 'human samples' to the Tokyo Army Medical College. The Kempeitai cremated human remains and disposed of them in the Sungari River. During 1942–4, Unit 731 was run by *Shosho* Professor Masaji Kitano who was replaced by epidemiologist *Chujo* Dr Shiro Ishii. Unit 731 came under direct orders of the *Rikugun-daijin Chujo* Sadao Araki who ensured through the Kempeitai that experimentation was not hampered.

Ishii was to organise four main centres of 'medical experiment'. At Anda, biological warfare bombs were tested and manufactured. During June–July 1942 the Japanese sprayed cholera, dysentery pathogens, plague and typhoid in the Jinhua area of China's Zhejiang Province using techniques pioneered at Anda. At

Changchun experiments took place on the spreading of anthrax and food poisoning. At Guangzhou prisoners were deliberately starved and human victims were experimented on with typhus and plague. Beijing's laboratories pursued means to dissolve bodies with chemicals. There were satellite facilities too at Malaya, various Chinese sites, Singapore and Hiroshima. Medical experiments were also carried out on Allied PoWs in the southeast Pacific. The 6th Field Kempeitai, under *Shosa* Kikuchi Satoru have been cited as playing a role in such experiments in this area.

At the end of the war Unit 731 and the satellite laboratories were destroyed and with the full cooperation of General Douglas MacArthur, Ishii was given immunity from prosecution in the War Crimes Trials. The information on his experiments given to the US government authorities was considered of too much value to be revealed in public. It is interesting to note that such perverted scientists as Ishii's head of vivisection, Hisato Yoshimura, taught at Japanese universities after the war. Military historian Richard Fuller (*Shokan*, 1992) averred that Ishii lectured in 'human testing of infectious organisms' at Fort Detrick, USA, in the late 1940s. *Shosho* Kitano was captured at Nanking in September 1945, but was also given immunity from war crime prosecution by the US Defense Department in exchange for surrendering research data.

In September 1997 former Kempeitai officer Yutaka Mio (b. 1914) admitted in Tokyo District Court that he had arrested Chinese citizens to be *maruta* for Unit 731; he is the first ex-Kempeitai to admit atrocities in a civil court. His testimony came about in a lawsuit first brought in 1995 by ten Chinese plaintiffs demanding £500,000 compensation from the Japanese government. Mio testified that to his knowledge his Kempeitai detachment alone sent 600 Chinese prisoners to their certain deaths at Unit 731. He averred to the court: 'Unit 731 was able to exist because of the Kempeitai. . . . Sending someone to Unit 731 was an act of murder.'

VI How the Kempeitai moved into occupied territory

The Philippines campaign is a good example of how Japan's military police integrated into a war zone. Kempeitai personnel, mostly drafted from Manchuquo duties, landed at Lingayen, the trading port and capital of Pangasinan Province, Luzon, on 20 December 1941. They entered Manila with the Imperial Japanese Army on 2 January 1942. Immediately, a headquarters was set up at the Jai Alai Club; the base was moved to Fort Santiago on 11 January. This Kempeitai organisation was to be called the Philippine Kempeitai Unit. Although there were to be thirty branches and detachments of Kempeitai throughout the provinces of the Philippines, the Philippine Kempeitai Unit was to be the central unit. Each Kempeitai detachment had a set area of operation, an HQ, a detachment commander and possibly a sub-station. Thus the Northern Manila detachment was based at the Far Eastern University, had a sub-station at the Wack-Wack Country Club and was commanded by *Tai-i* Takefumi Fujita. During the period of Japanese occupation there were to be three successive Kempeitai Commanders-in-Chief: December 1941–October 1942, *Chusa* Seichi Ohta; October 1942–February 1945, *Taisa* Akira Nagahama; and February–September 1945, *Shosho* Kenshichi Matsuoka. In reality, though, the Kempeitai branches outside Manila were actively controlled for the most part by the army garrisons. By October 1942 there were around 150 Kempeitai personnel in Manila and 300 in the provinces, and an NCO Kempeitai training school was established at Intramuros, Manila. This brought the Kempeitai strength up to 1,800 by June 1944, with recruitment from the Army in the Philippines and China.

The main duties of the Kempeitai in the Philippines were to discipline army personnel and Japanese civilians in the area; gather military intelligence; arrest civilians who violated military codes; watch out for deserters; inspect boats arriving at

Philippine ports; check communications being made by US forces; round up suspected guerrillas; counter anti-Japanese ideology; seek out and impound wireless equipment; and maintain peace and order. The implementation of the latter duty always left much to be desired. Each overall commander had his own idiosyncratic priorities for duties; in the case of *Taisa* Ohta this was countering the looting of Philippine houses by the Army – in this he was a singular failure.

Throughout the Philippines Japanese soldiers behaved abominably to all they encountered: homes were violated, women raped, innocent civilians beaten up for no reason and bayonets prodded at those who did not salute or bow. Nevertheless, Japanese soldiers were admonished by the Kempeitai for excesses, particularly in detachment areas like Iloide (*Tai-i* Kaneyoki Koike) and Bagiuo (*Shosa* Kazuo Fukutake), where the Kempeitai wished to build up good relationships to facilitate intelligence gathering. Otherwise they turned a blind eye, and even destroyed charge sheets on Japanese military personnel.

Inherent problem areas for the Philippine Kempeitai were money forging, the activities of usurers, and impersonation. The forging of Occupation Currency 'disturbed the economic welfare of the country' thundered the *Official Journal of the Japanese Military Administration*. And, when this administration agreed that ethnic banknotes should rank equally with Occupation Currency, money changers such as Jesús María Ciu and Ko Chiang mopped up old banknotes at ridiculously low prices and undermined the Occupation Currency's face value. Many an impostor such as the Chinese Wang Ku, donned Kempeitai insignia and 'confiscated' goods for resale, or operated protection rackets.

Guerrilla and sabotage groups were always a problem to the Kempeitai in the Philippines. In particular *Taisa* Akira Nagahama mounted a 'killing orgy' against guerrilla leader Lt-Col. Pabling Jornacio, leading to 'inhuman and barbarous acts' against the inhabitants of Eastern Laguna and Eastern Rizal. Many areas which the Kempeitai considered to be the lairs of guerrillas ('abodes of hostile elements' in Kempeitai jargon) were 'zonified' for regular searches, ransackings, torturings and executions.

The Philippine Kempeitai units were also particularly active in disseminating propaganda with Taisa Nagahama writing articles in the Manila Tribune on such themes as 'The Filipinos are not a conquered race and the Japanese are not conquerors', or 'The Filipinos must forget the "unwholesome influences" of America and collaborate wholeheartedly with Japan'. Propaganda was targeted against guerrillas. Censorship of films, drama, newspapers and mail was severe.

The need to establish a competent intelligence network in the Philippines forced the Kempeitai to employ both local and foreign informers. This was mainly because the Kempeitai did not speak English or the many native dialects. Kempeitai personnel on espionage duty were usually accompanied by an interpreter. Kempeitai informers included native collaborators, groups of criminals, pimps, prostitutes and outlaws, pro-Japanese Philippine Constabulary officers and pro-Axis foreigners (Germans, Italians and Spanish) including diplomatic staff like the Falangist José del Costano, the Spanish consul at Manila. According to Philippine War Crimes Trials documents, some Filipino collaborators were trained as Kempeitai soldiers with temporary ranks to enhance their enthusiasm as local informers. Kempeitai informers ran great personal risks of discovery, or of being suspected as double agents.

In time the word Kempeitai became synonymous in the Philippines with the word torture, and Kempeitai arrest meant certain death. Most Kempeitai detachment centres had their own prison complexes of varying barbarity. The most notorious was Fort Santiago, Manila, dubbed 'The Bastille of Pasig' (the local river), with its twelve hell-hole cells. Here both high and low, native and foreigner underwent physical and mental torture at the behest of the Kempeitai. Escape from Fort Santiago was deemed impossible; even to try earned the perpetrator bayoneting to the floor through the feet and then beheading. Yet, one man succeeded, to become a hero of the Kempeitai years in the Philippines. Marciel P. Lichauco recalls the hero in *Dear Mother Putnam* (1949).

A dentist, Dr Vincente M. Domingo, was arrested and tortured by the Kempeitai on a charge of aiding guerrillas. He confessed that he owned a pistol (an illegal act) and that it was in a safe in his surgery. Handcuffed, Domingo was taken to the surgery by three Kempeitai officers and an interpreter to retrieve the pistol. Once at the surgery Domingo persuaded his captors to unhandcuff him while he opened the safe's combination. This they did and Domingo opened the safe, turned and flung a bundle of banknotes on to a nearby table with the invitation to the soldiers to divide them up among themselves. As they did so he retrieved the pistol and in a skilful piece of shooting killed the soldiers; the interpreter fled. Domingo escaped, never to be captured again.

CHAPTER THREE

MAYHEM AND MURDER
IN MANCHURIA

The arrogance of the Japanese in Manchuria especially of the officers of the Imperial Japanese Army, is developing an immeasurable hatred amongst all classes of the population. This is caused by the fact that the worst civil and military elements, whose one motive is to amass a fortune in the shortest time possible, and who resort to every method of oppression to attain their purpose, are sent to Manchuria. They extort money from the people and compel farmers to plant poppies instead of soya beans.

Yoshiko Kawashima, Chinese secret service agent,
Radio broadcast, 1934

Roughly comprising the modern provinces of Heilongjiang, Jilin and Liaoning, Manchuria is a region of North East China bordering the Russian Federation. It was known to the Chinese as Tung San Sheng and today as Dongbei. To the east and west, the region is mountainous and has a large central fertile plain. In the late nineteenth century this productive area was dominated by Czarist Russia, the Russians having forced the Chinese in November 1860 to cede to them the whole of east-coast Manchuria from the Amur River to the Yalu River. This territory became known as *Primorsk* (Maritime Province of the Empire of the Russias). When China lost the war with Japan (1894–5), the vast, crumbling empire of the Manchus became a picking ground for imperialist powers. By the Treaty of Shimonoseki (1895), Japan took Port Arthur, Formosa, the Pescadores and other strategic locations. Japanese expansionist aims meant that eyes were then cast on Manchuria in particular, which led to the conflict of the Russo-Japanese War (1904–5).

The Imperial Czarist Fleet under Admiral Zinovy Petrovich Rozhdestvenski was routed by *Taisho Hakushaku* (Admiral Count) Heihachiro Togo at the Battle of Tsushima Strait. By the Treaty of Portsmouth (New Hampshire, USA, 23 August 1905), Japan won concessions which meant that she would not be constrained in her move against Manchuria. On 18 September 1931 the Japanese manufactured the *Manshu Jihen* (Manchurian Incident) by firing on Chinese soldiers who they claimed had tried to sabotage the South Manchurian Railway. Japan's action violated the Kellog-Briand 'outlawry of war' Pact of 27 August 1928 and the subsequent occupation of Manchuria by the Guangdong (Kwangtung) Army set Japan on a course for *Dai ni-ji Sekai Taisen* (the Second World War).

During 18 February 1932 the Japanese set up a puppet state of ten administrative provinces in Manchuria in an attempt to legitimise the new regime. The most senior Japanese military officer acted as Japan's ambassador, with an added portfolio to negotiate for Japan's much needed raw materials, and the consolidation of the country's security position against the USSR. The Japanese occupation of Manchuria brought many new industrial products to North East China to supplement the traditional trade in gold, gingseng and furs. The Japanese established such new industrial towns as Kanseishi. Manchuria was re-named Manchuquo (Land of the Manchus) by the Japanese after 1932; and in 1933 the province of Jehol (Chengde) was annexed to Manchuquo. The country was diplomatically isolated until the Manchuquo-German Trade Agreement of April 1936. Italy recognised the country in 1937 and Germany in 1938. Nationalist China never formally recognised Manchuquo, but

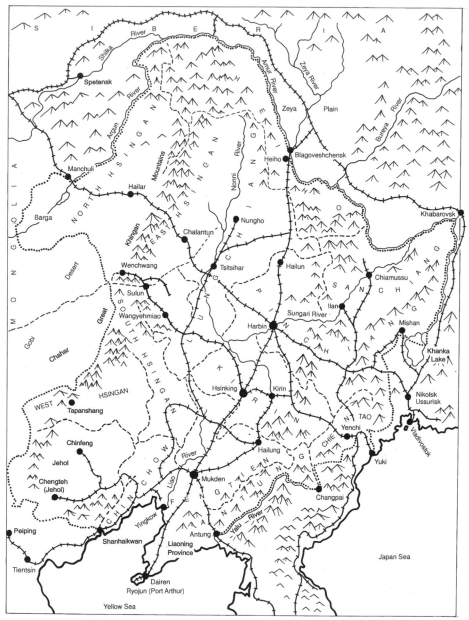

Manchuquo of the Japanese

The old Manchurian town of Changchun became the new capital of Manchuquo under the name of Hsingking (Xinjing) in Chinese and Shinkyo in Japanese. The Kempeitai headquarters was in the new capital, with strong presences at Ryojun (Port Arthur), Dairen, Mukden and Harbin.

His Imperial Majesty, Pu Yi, Emperor of China, 1908–12. Here dressed in state uniform as Emperor of Manchuquo, Pu Yi ruled the Japanese puppet state during 1935–45, propped up militarily by the Imperial Japanese Army and the Kempeitai. Born in 1906 he died in 1967. (JRP)

those for whom it was useful to do so, such as the political defector Wang Ching-wei in Nanking, paid lip service to its legitimacy.

The Japanese installed as 'chief executive' of Manchuquo a political pawn called Henry Pu Yi. The grand-nephew of the Dowager Empress Tz'u-hsi, Henry Pu Yi had succeeded to the Peacock Throne of China at the age of three in 1908 as the last Manchu emperor of the Ch'ing Dynasty. He was deposed in 1911 after the Republican revolution but was temporarily restored by the leaders of the Peiyang warlord clique in 1917. For years Henry Pu Yi was to live a time-warped existence in the Forbidden City, the name for the imperial palace and its buildings in central Peking. Henry Pu Yi was ousted from the Forbidden City by General Yu-hsiang Feng, army commander with the Chihli warlord forces at the occupation of Peking on 23 October 1924. Henry Pu Yi was encouraged to take up residence at the Japanese Legation under the protection of Minister Yoshizawa, head of the Japanese diplomatic mission. More and more he came under Japanese influence and willingly agreed to lead the new administration at Manchuquo.

A key player in the placement of Henry Pu Yi was *Shosho* Kenji Doihara, Director of the Military Intelligence Bureau at Mukden (Shenyang), capital of Liaoning Province. Doihara was a fluent Chinese-speaking, skilled 'old China hand' and was thoroughly experienced in subversive techniques. He had been selected to shoehorn Henry Pu Yi firmly into position with the ultimate aim of making him emperor of China once more, but this time under strict Japanese control. Henry Pu Yi was installed as 'chief executive' in 1932 and was promoted to Emperor of Manchuquo in March 1934, under the name of Kang Te. Changchun (Xinjing; Shinkyo to the Japanese) was selected as the puppet emperor's new capital, to be hedged in with Kempeitai.

The 'independence' of the state of Manchuquo was a complete

Kempeitai Propaganda & Disinformation

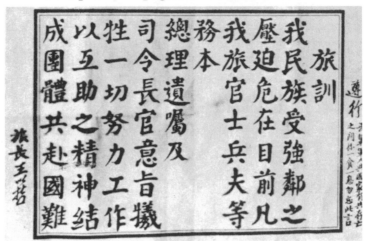

Forged anti-Japanese leaflet, 1930s, Manchuquo. The calligraphy reads: 'The oppression of [our] powerful neighbour being upon us, danger is at hand. Arise, our men! Do your utmost in emergency.' The text is purported to be signed by Maj.-Gen. Wang-iche, a prominent brigade commander of the Chinese Army.

Kempeitai poster printed to fly-post Chinese military barracks to encourage the protection of Japanese-administered Manchuquo Railway property. The calligraphy reads: 'Keep a watch on the railway to the west of our barracks.'

sham intended to hoodwink the League of Nations into believing that the Japanese had no role to play in its administration; no one was fooled. The Japanese forced the Chinese who were in the employ of the old Manchurian government to remain to give the impression that the people had invited the Japanese to protect them from the Chinese Kuomintang Party, the Bolsheviks and the indigenous Chinese bandits. The Kuomintang had been organised in 1912 following the overthrow of the imperial government, from revolutionary Dr Sun Yat Sen's Alliance Society. It formed an accommodation in 1924 with the Chinese Communist Party, and following Sun's death was led by Chiang Kai-shek. By 1926 the Communist Party had wrested control of most of China away from the warlords. The two parties split in 1927, a situation which incited a civil war that persisted until the Japanese conquests, which led ultimately to renewed cooperation in 1937. When the Japanese set up Manchuquo the Kuomintang formed their own secret service, called the Tung Meng Hui Club, to monitor Kempeitai and Japanese intelligence activity.

Manchuquo became a playground, training area and killing field for the Kempeitai. By 1932 there were 150,000 Japanese soldiers in Manchuquo, alongside 18,000 Kempeitai and 400 secret service agents (in effect civilian Kempeitai). Some of Japan's most influential Kempeitai officers and prominent wartime leaders were to cut their teeth and enhance their notoriety in Manchuquo.

Among such officers these may be mentioned. During 1932–4, *Chujo* Taranosuke Hashimoto was commander of the Manchuquo Kempeitai; he went on to become *Jikan Rikugun-daijin* in 1934. *Shosho* Shizuichi Tanaka became Commander of the Kwantung Army Kempeitai in Manchuria in August 1937. Incidentally, the Kwantung Army (*Kantogun* in Japanese), Japan's field army in Manchuquo, had been created on 1 August 1916 by Japanese forces occupying southern Manchuria after the Russo-Japanese War.

Tanaka was promoted to *Chujo* and Commander of the Kempeitai, Tokyo, in July 1938 and remained in that position until 1940. His Kempeitai experience and influence took him to the rank of Commander-in-Chief of Japan's Eastern District Army. *Shosa* Ryoji Shikata's career move to become Commander of the Tokyo Kempeitai (1941–4), was to be built on his earlier experience as aide-de-camp to one of Japan's most celebrated Kempeitai officers; indeed, no one was more ruthless or influential than *Taisho* Hideki Tojo.

Until 1938 Hideki '*Kamisori*' ('the Razor') Tojo was virtually unknown internationally, and even in Japan. Yet he was to rise to be dictator of Japan and *Sori-daijin* at the time of the military attack the Japanese call *Shinjuwan Kogeki* (the assault on Pearl Harbor). An insensate hater of *gaijin*, Tojo was archetypal among the Japanese militarists who made themselves masters of Japan in the 1930s. Although the Army was divided in itself into various factions like the *Kodo-hu* (Imperial Way School) and the *Tosei-hu* (Central School – which Tojo supported), the overall consensus was a despising of party politics and a contempt for democracy. The end of old party government was achieved by the Army in 1932.

Tojo was born on 30 December 1884 into a (low caste) *samurai* family devoted to the largely misunderstood – in the West – military code of *Bushido* ('The Way of the Warrior'). This code of chivalry, called 'The Soul of Japan' by its most famous interpreter Dr Inazo Nitobe, and through which the *samurai* cultivated martial virtues and were indifferent to death or pain in their loyalty to the *daimyo*, was to be dragged through the pestilence of dishonour by the Kempeitai in the Second World War. There was no greater perverter of *Bushido* than Tojo.

In 1902 Hideki Tojo entered the infantry branch of the Military Academy; he was commissioned *Chu-i* in August 1905, and immediately took up garrison duty in Manchuria to serve until 1906, the year he was promoted to *Tai-i*. Staff college followed

Hideki Tōjo (1884–1948), bearing insignia of the rank of Taisa, c. 1912. In 1935 he became Commander of the Kwangtung Army Kempeitai in Manchuquo; he was to remain a loyal supporter of the Kempeitai throughout his military/political career. He rose to be Taisho and Sori-daijin in 1940. Indicted on fifty counts as a Class A War Criminal, he was executed by hanging. (JRP)

until 1915; thereafter as *Taisa* he served for a while in Siberia, rounding off with General Staff and regimental duties by the end of the First World War. During 1919–22 Tojo was Military Attaché at the Japanese Embassy in Berlin and thereafter an instructor at the Military Staff College, Tokyo; by August 1924 he was promoted *Chusa*. During the early 1930s he served variously as Battalion Commander of the 1st Infantry Regiment and Head of the General Affairs Bureau of the *Rikugunsho* as *Shosho* (1933). Tojo progressed to be Commandant of the Military Academy, and Commander of the 24th Infantry Brigade, Kyushu main island, by 1934. Now began his association with the Kempeitai for in October 1935 he became Commander of the Japanese Kwangtung Army Kempeitai in Manchuquo. Tojo, incidentally, served in this capacity until 1937, when he was replaced by *Shosho* Keisuke Fujii, then Chief of the General Affairs Bureau (Kempeitai HQ Kwangtung Army).

Manchuquo was run by a consortium of local civilian officials, businessmen, Kempeitai officers and their stooges, and army officers, with the final say in all matters in the hands of *Chujo* Seishiro Itagaki, Chief of Staff of the Kwangtung Army. A man with blood on his hands – he had been involved in the murder of Chinese warlord and Governor-General of Manchuria, Marshal Chang Tso-lin in 1928 – Itagaki was a key player in the Manchurian Incident alongside the then *Shosa* Kenji Ishihara.

From his first days in Manchuquo, Tojo showed all who came in contact with him that he considered his Kempeitai the only permitted body of law enforcement, and no more bloody, ruthless, morally rotten force existed anywhere. Tojo built on the reality that his role made him responsible for all aspects of security, and that his remit was capable of wide interpretation. He built up a comprehensive set of dossiers on private and public activities which might be deemed dangerous to the Japanese authorities. It is clear that Tojo was not setting up a secret police network like the *Geheimstaatspolizei* (1933) of *Schutzstaffel* (SS)

Chief Heinrich Himmler in Germany. Yet in Army-administered Manchuquo, where Chinese intrigue was a way of life and Japanese security was obsessive, a type of police state was inevitable.

Over and above the Army Kempeitai there were some 100,000 Japanese 'advisers' under their influence. There was not a department, office or company that did not have such an 'adviser', recruited largely by the Kempeitai – and other Japanese authorities – from Japanese civilians already in Manchuquo and who could speak Chinese and Russian.

These civilians were a mixed band of felons and adventurers, drug-pushers and brothel-keepers, whom the Kempeitai protected under the *Hinomaru* (Japanese national flag) and embassy extra-territorial rights, to keep them outside the reach of the Chinese courts. The 'advisers' existed mostly on the proceeds of the criminal gains and through 'protection money' from wealthy Chinese and Russian businesses. The Kempeitai actively imported undesirables and criminals released on general amnesty by the emperor from mainland Japan to top up their network of 'advisers'.

A typical Japanese 'adviser' and Kempeitai stooge was Konstantin Ivanovich Nakamura, a Japanese national who had embraced the Russian Orthodox religion. A barber by trade, Nakamura had lived in Korea and Manchuria since before the First World War and ran a barber's shop at Nahaloika, a suburb of Harbin (modern capital of Heilongjian Province), the important railway centre which was a relic of Old Russia. The shop was a front to sell morphine, heroin and opium, and Nakamura ran a brothel a few yards down the street. His activities were known to the Chinese authorities, who also knew to turn a blind eye. Three times, though, Nakamura was brought before the Japanese-run courts and the mode of his absolution shows how the law was manipulated by the Kempeitai in these cases through the Japanese *ryoji* (consul).

In Japanese puppet states the Kempeitai were charged with seeking out coin counterfeiters. In particular they monitored the coinage of Hopei, China (left: obverse 10 cents copper-nickel issue 1937), and Manchuquo (right: obverse, flag motif, bronze 1933–4 issue). (JRP)

Japanese records show that in 1923 Nakamura had contracted an illegal marriage to a Russian widow with an eleven-year-old daughter. Nakamura sexually assaulted the girl, and after a complaint to the Chinese authorities by the mother he was arrested and handed over to the *ryoji*. The Kempeitai lawyer pointed out that according to Japanese law, which applied, Nakamura had 'bought' the girl when he 'bought' (illegally married) the mother. As he had assaulted her on his private property, he was not therefore liable to prosecution.

In 1926 Nakamura was accused of drugging a Russian national in his barber's shop and robbing him of $500. The Russian complained to the police. The Kempeitai intervened and told the *ryoji* that the man had not been drugged but had been drunk and had imagined the whole thing. Nakamura was released. In 1928 the Kempeitai saved Nakamura again when he was found to be using twelve-year-old girls in his brothel. Nakamura rose to become chief 'adviser' to the Kempeitai in Harbin.

One commentator who first informed the West about Kempeitai activity in Manchuquo in particular was Signor Amleto Vespa. In 1931 the 43-year-old Italian was an ex-mercenary of General Francisco Madera's Mexican Revolutionary Army and a freelance journalist who had been recruited by the Allied Intelligence Service of the First World War. As a businessman in Manchuria he had been forced, through threats to his family's safety, to work for the Japanese Secret Service. Vespa left a record of Kempeitai activities in Manchuquo in his *Secret Agent of Japan* (1938), as well as comment about Chinese intelligence.

Once a very effective force the Chinese Secret Service of Amleto Vespa's day was no match for the Kempeitai. In the library of Kempeitai HQ at Tokyo was a volume by the Chinese author Sun Tzu (*Sonshi* to the Japanese). Entitled *Ping Fa* ('Principles of War'), it remains the earliest known volume on espionage, and the arts of war, and dates from *c.* 510 BC. Thus from these early days the various Chinese kingdoms had had an espionage system. The decaying, reactionary and feudal court of the nineteenth century Manchu rulers, however, led to China having an ineffective Secret Service which assisted the ultimate break-up of the Chinese empire. Corruption and bribery prevented the self-seeking Chinese intelligence chiefs from safeguarding China's interests and slowly the west dismantled Chinese hegemony in the Orient.

The United States government, in particular, encouraged Japan to occupy the Chinese-inhabited Liu Chiu Islands (now Okinawa) in 1871, and attack Formosa (Taiwan). While the British seized Burma and the French took Vietnam in the mid-1850s, the Japanese expanded their espionage system in the Orient and the network was to be manipulated in due course by the Kempeitai.

One of the main difficulties the Japanese government agents and

Italian diplomat Amleto Vespa with Taisa and Madam Tanaka at Tientsin in 1929. Tanaka was Chief of Japanese Intelligence and a prominent Kempeitai linkman in pre-Second World War China. Vespa was one of the first to write about Kempeitai atrocities committed in China and Manchuria for the western press in the late 1930s. (JRP)

the Kempeitai encountered in modern espionage was that their native-born agents were easily spotted because of their racial characteristics. So they began to employ Europeans to spy for them. One such was the British double agent Sigismund Georgievich Rosenblum, later to be called Sydney Reilly. By 1908 the Manchu Secret Service was almost non-existent and Reilly's information about this convinced the Japanese that the Chinese empire was foundering and that they must act soon to get their share of the pickings. Thus, when Amleto Vespa began to work for the Japanese, the Chinese Secret Service was considered a joke at Kempeitai HQ.

Amleto Vespa testified that the Kempeitai encouraged their 'advisers' to assault any 'enemies' in Manchuquo. They incited bands of the depraved to beat up and rob Chinese and Russian businessmen. These bands were nicknamed *ronin* after the masterless *samurai* of old who gained a living by hiring themselves out as swordsmen. It was a slur on the memory of many ancient *ronin* who had appeared honourably in Japan's history and literature. These Manchuquo *ronin* extracted 'protection money' from Chinese and Russian cafés, restaurants and bars, turning up to eat and drink large quantities without paying. It was a pattern also followed by their Kempeitai masters who looted café owners' gramophones, radios and furniture at will.

White women were particularly prone to assault, rape and public abuse in Japanese Manchuquo. One raped woman, averred Vespa, who complained to the Kempeitai on duty at the *Nippon Ryojikan* at Harbin was raped again by Kempeitai officers, arrested and placed in a Chinese jail on a charge of 'practising prostitution'. It was a common occurrence. When Russian papers began to report such assaults the Kempeitai ordered – on penalty of the newspapers being shut down – that the news items should not use the word Japanese when suspects were being described – they had to substitute 'foreigners' as guilty parties. Harbin sported two English language newspapers, the *Harbin Herald* and the

Harbin Observer. The former was edited by British journalist Lenox Simpson. He regularly criticised the Japanese authorities in general, and the Kempeitai in particular, in his columns. Eventually the Kempeitai confiscated his type and presses and he was expelled.

From a new base at the port of Dairen, he began proceedings to achieve redress. He petitioned the House of Lords. The British Foreign Office complained to Tokyo via the Japanese Embassy in London, but the Japanese government refused to agree compensation. B. Haydon Fleet, editor of the *Harbin Observer*, never criticised the Japanese in his columns, but the Kempeitai hounded him and he left for Shanghai to direct the Fleet News Agency. The Kempeitai and general Japanese propaganda were served through the Russian language papers in Harbin, the *Harbinskoe Vremia* and the anti-semitic White Russian *Nash Put*.

It was common knowledge that a posting to Manchuquo was a great perk for Kempeitai officers. Through looting and extortion, individuals could become rich. They set up drug, sex and gambling monopolies, franchising them out for huge fees. Another lucrative Kempeitai activity was the kidnapping of wealthy people for ransom; because the Kempeitai were held in such fear ransoms were usually promptly paid. As the Kempeitai controlled the Customs of Manchuquo they did their utmost to prevent non-Japanese goods entering the country, even sabotaging cargoes in customs warehouses. The best foreign goods were regularly stolen by the Kempeitai and sent back to Japan free via the Chinese Eastern Railway then run by a Sino-Russian consortium. It was estimated that during a two- to three-year tour of duty a Kempeitai officer could amass $50,000 to $100,000.

Not every Japanese commander in Manchuria approved of Kempeitai methods and corruption. One such was *Taisho* Nobuyoshi Muto, who by 1932 was proconsul at the former seat

The Kempeitai sponsored and promoted cheap drug dens in the Occupied Territories to undermine native resistance. In Manchuquo in particular several Kempeitai officers became rich through dealing in opiates. Here a victim of Kempeitai indulgence slumps outside a Chinese opium den in filth and rags. (JRP)

of Manchu government at Mukden (modern Shengyang, capital of Liaoning Province) and special *taishi* to Manchuquo. He endeavoured to use the Japanese Secret Service to report on Kempeitai excesses in an attempt to curb them and to have the worst perpetrators repatriated to Japan. He prepared a report for the *Rikugunsho* on the matter which was 'lost' in the Japanese bureaucratic system. At length he made a personal appeal to Emperor Hirohito concerning the excesses, underlining his intent by committing *seppuku* (ritual suicide) on 27 July 1933. Hirohito took no action and the Kempeitai continued untrammelled.

Kempeitai reports to both territorial HQ and Tokyo were generally travesties of the truth. One such concerned the case of Kempeitai soldier Shintaro Kakehei. The scene was a street in Harbin. It was evening. Kakehei stopped a Russian and endeavoured to search him. The Russian, fired up with vodka, grabbed Kakehei by the collar, took his revolver, and beat him to the point where the officer had a cracked skull and a broken arm. The Russian was arrested by Sub-Inspector Feodorov of the Harbin Criminal Department who made a report on the incident. The Harbin Kempeitai commander was enraged at Feodorov's report, suggesting as it did that a drunken Russian could beat up a Kempeitai officer; it was an insult to the emperor. Feodorov was forced to sign a new report for Kempeitai HQ. The report was preserved by Amleto Vespa:

On the evening of 5 June 1933, at 10 pm, [Kempeitai officer] Shintaro Kakehei met a group of more than 20 young Communists who were shouting and outraging peaceful citizens, thus disturbing the public peace; [Kempeitai officer] Kakehei courageously faced the group of Communists and ordered them to disperse and stop causing scandals. The drunken Communists . . . fell upon him and beat him with sticks.

[Kempeitai] Kakehei, like a true *samurai*, defended himself with admirable courage and, although seriously hurt, succeeded in repelling the Communists, arresting the leader and placing him in the custody of [Sub-Inspector Feodorov]. His duty thus accomplished he fainted.

Three months after the incident Kakehei received a commendation for his 'valour' and Feodorov was congratulated for his report.

In Manchuquo the Kempeitai also exploited the extant Chinese secret societies, but one of their own was to prove invaluable. Called in Japanese the *Kokuryukai*, the 'Black Dragon Society' (which took its name from the Chinese characters for the Amur River), it had among its members many Imperial Japanese Army officers, blackmailers, *soshi* ('brave knights', i.e. unemployed *samurai*), hired killers, secret agents, thugs and cabinet ministers. Although the *Kokuryukai* was to operate from Korea to the USA, at first their work was mainly in Manchuquo and Russia, and in the former military attachés and senior Kempeitai were usually appointed with their approval. One such was *Taisa* Motojiro Akashi, later Commander-in-Chief of the Kempeitai and Chief-of-Staff of the Army in Korea. He had links with the OKHRANA. It was Akashi who recruited Sidney Reilly.

The Kempeitai met their match in the Chinese bandits. These were variously religious fanatics, anti-Japanese guerrillas, anti-government dissidents, dispossessed peasants and followers of the deposed warlord Cheng Hsueh-liang. By 1933 there were some 65,000 of them in Manchuquo. The bandits regularly succeeded in blowing up Japanese military trains, sabotaging Japanese installations and picking off Kempeitai agents. Kempeitai retribution was swift and bestial. In the case of the Japanese military train dynamited by bandits near Hengtaohotze, west of Muling, in which 192 Japanese soldiers died and 374 were injured, the Kempeitai arrested 400 innocent Chinese and Russians of all ages and sexes for interrogation. Most were executed and the 'investigation' was

Hundreds of innocent Chinese were executed by the Kempeitai as Japan tightened its grip on mainland China. Victims' heads are publicly displayed here at a Chinese town to warn others against resistance. (JRP)

rounded off by the harrying of the surrounding countryside. As a Kempeitai officer was to remark: 'Only with terror can we teach these Russians and Chinese anything.' In truth, by 1937 the Japanese only controlled the districts of Manchuquo contiguous with the railway system; a few yards from the lines the bandits held sway.

On 9 May 1932 the League of Nations sent a mission to Manchuquo to study reports on Japanese aggression; it was chaired by the British statesman Victor Alexander George Robert Bulwer-Lytton, who had been Governor of Bengal, 1922–7. In the weeks prior to the visit the Kempeitai tightened their control of, or links with, the independently operating police agencies within Manchuquo. At the time they included: the Japanese Secret Service; the State Police of old Manchuria, under the Ministry of the Interior; the City Police, Harbin; the Japanese Consular Police; the Manchurian Criminal Police of the Municipal Authorities; the old Manchurian State Intelligence Service; and the Railway Police. The Kempeitai ordered all of the police bodies to root out and arrest any who might give adverse reports to the commission; they were to be held for up to forty days after the commission departed. Records show that 1,361 suspects were rounded up and sent to a Kempeitai detention camp at Sunbei, across the Sungari River from Harbin. All political prisoners already in custody were also removed to Sunbei, as were all hospital patients who could speak English or French. Nothing was left to chance.

A month before the commission arrived, the Japanese authorities had ordered a number of influential Chinese and Russians to sign 'petitions', written by Japanese lawyers, detailing how well, legally and generously the Japanese ruled Manchuquo. A reception committee was also hand-picked and briefed and made word perfect. The commission members were to stay at Harbin's Hotel Moderne, whose staff were all selected by the Kempeitai. In case commission members elected to stay at other hotels such as the Grand and the Novi Mir, their staffs were planted too.

The Kempeitai also ensured that each household should display Manchuquo flags and pictures of Chief Executive Henry Pu Yi. Each house was checked by a Kempeitai officer to see that the emblems were in position. A Kempeitai soldier was also placed at the private residences of all who had any semblance of wealth or influence. Yet while the commission was in town no Kempeitai uniform was to be seen, to reinforce the pretence that the Japanese were only visitors and not occupiers of the country.

Only one incident marred the arrival of the commission. As they descended from their train members were accosted by a Kempeitai agent, a Korean called Kim Kwok, who attempted to present a petition to Lord Lytton. In it he asked why the commission were so interested in Manchuquo as the Japanese had only been there a short time, while his homeland had been occupied by the Japanese for years. Kwok was hustled away by Kempeitai soldiers, who beat and tortured him to extract information about his (non-existent) accomplices. Kwok was shot when he refused to talk.

Each commission member was assigned four Kempeitai agents to mount a round the clock 'guard', their presence being explained as protection against communist assassination attempts. However, despite Kempeitai precautions, a large number of Manchurian Chinese, Russians and Koreans succeeded in getting messages to the commission members and Lord Lytton was able to incorporate their opinions in his report to the League.

Internationally the Japanese let it be known that they cared not a jot what the League of Nations thought of them. Yet when the commission report was published the Japanese reaction was one of hysterical fury. The Kempeitai, in particular, displayed anger that their hard work to gag the critics of Manchuquo had largely failed. The commission report underlined the fact that the

Japanese were two-timing aggressors. In 1933 Japan withdrew from the League.

In Manchuquo the Kempeitai were to target the *yudaya-jin* (Jews), although in the philosophy of the military police there was a certain ambivalence towards the Jews. For most Japanese emerging from their feudal purdah, the differences between Jew and Gentile were hardly readily apparent, or relevant. Then in 1904 they found that they needed to borrow money on the international market to continue their war with Russia. Turned down for the full amount they required by London bankers, they were able to borrow all they needed through a $200 million deal between the Vice-Governor of the *Nihon Ginko* (Bank of Japan), *Danshaku* Korekiyo Takahashi, and Jacob Schiff, a partner in the US investment bank of Kuhn-Loeb. Thus the usefulness of financial Jewry made itself known to the Japanese in general with Schiff as a guest of Emperor Meiji at the *Kyujo*.

Japan's military intellectuals saw much to praise in the Jews whom they believed to have brought about the laudable downfall of the Russian, German and Austro-Hungarian Empires during the First World War; yet after that war the seeds of anti-semitism were sewn in Japan's military circles. (As the Jewish population in Japan has never exceeded 1,000, anti-semitism has hardly been registered in Japanese society in general.) Then in 1919 Japanese soldiers went off to fight alongside the White Russians in Siberia. There they encountered the rabid anti-semite General Gregorii Semonov. The general gave each Japanese soldier a copy of a book called *The Protocols of the Elders of Zion*, which alleged with the utmost virulence how Jews were bent on world domination. The Japanese who read the book took the contents to be the literal truth.

Two Japanese were to become 'experts on Jewry' on the initial strength of their absorption of the *Protocols*; one was *Tai-i* Norihito Yasue, a Russian-language specialist on Semonov's staff, and the other was a naval officer, Koreshige Inuzuka. They were the first of a pool of such 'experts' who monitored diplomatic studies of Jewry worldwide (on the orders of the *Gaimusho*) and drew up a list of prominent Jews in countries which interested them. The Kempeitai were to use these lists for their own purposes in Manchuquo.

At first the Jews in old Manchuria were granted legal status to conduct their community businesses and affairs. By the mid-1920s there were 13,000 Russian Jews in Harbin, Hailar, Tsitsihar, Manchuli, Mukden and Dairen. Their leaders were Dr Abraham Kaufman and Rabbi Aaron Kiselef, who helped organise Jewish schools, hospitals, banks and so on. When it became clear that the Jews were potential financial milch cows, the Kempeitai began to target them, kidnapping victims and extorting ransoms. One such kidnapping was to be known throughout the international gossip network in China as 'The Simon Kaspé Case'.

Simon was the son of the wealthy Russian Jew Joseph Kaspé, theatrical entrepreneur and owner of the Hotel Moderne. The young man was a talented musician and was at home for the summer vacation in August 1933 when, one evening while returning home with his girlfriend, he was attacked and kidnapped. Next morning Kaspé senior was sent a ransom note for $100,000.

As a naturalised French citizen, and on the advice of his country's consul, Kaspé refused to pay. The consul set about finding Simon with the cooperation of the Kempeitai who played a double game. Thirty days were to pass with no success, when Joseph Kaspé received a portion of a human ear purporting to be that of his son. Again the consul advised non-payment of the ransom. On 3 December 1933 the Japanese authorities found Simon Kaspé's body; he had been beaten, starved, tortured and mutilated, and had been kept for most of his ninety-five days of captivity in an underground pit in freezing conditions. The young man had been finally shot. Simon Kaspé's funeral was attended by thousands of the horrified population. As he was lowered into his grave there were angry shouts of 'Death to the Kempeitai', 'Down with the Imperial Japanese Army'.

The Jewish communities of Harbin and Shanghai protested to Japan's *Jiken Gaimu-daijin* Mamoru Shigemitsu. Their efforts were in vain. The Kempeitai stooges who had killed Simon Kaspé were apprehended and jailed, but were released on probation. Even though the kidnappers were brought to trial and convicted, the Kempeitai arrested the Chinese judges and prosecuted them for treason. A re-trial was carried out with Japanese judges; the kidnappers were given ten- to fifteen-year sentences, but were released under an amnesty one week later.

Following the Kaspé outrage thousands of Jews fled Manchuquo, which put in jeopardy a plan which was just evolving. By 1932 it was important for Japan to populate outlying areas of Manchuquo against the incursions of Russian and Outer-Mongolian troops. A target of one million households were to be shipped from Japan to resettle in Manchuquo to populate the region of the Sungari River and the Russian Maritime Province. A large portion of the menfolk were designed to be army reservists. The Kempeitai were assigned the support role of removing any indigenous Chinese from the chosen settlement areas. Peasants and landowners were to resist in large numbers and many were supported by bandit groups. The Kempeitai resorted to strong-arm tactics (and the bombing of villages) in troubles that were to continue until the opening of the Second World War. Into this milieu the Japanese planned to relocate Jews.

From 1934 to 1940 the Japanese government devised a policy known as the Fugu Plan, which sought to involve both European and US Jewry in the building up of Japan's empire. The plan to offer a 'safe haven' from anti-semitism to 50,000 Jews in Manchuquo was the idea of *Chujo* Kiichiro Higuchi, Chief of the Military Mission in Manchuquo. In reality the plan was doomed from the outset because of Japan's misunderstanding of the nature, culture and politics of the Jewish people, and of the effectiveness in the Japanese mind of the anti-semitic propaganda stemming from Hitler's National Socialists. To this was added the anti-Jewish policy of the Kempeitai in Manchuquo.

Jewry was linked with Freemasonry in Japanese eyes and the Kempeitai peddled the propaganda that 'The League of Nations is a tool of the Jewish financiers'. Masao Kubota wrote in *Masho no Kugutsushi Furimeisen* ('Devilish Puppeteers, Freemasons'): 'By founding the League of Nations, freemasons formed a world state government.' Thus, in Manchuquo the Kempeitai looked upon Freemasonry as a Jewish organisation, a secret society and a source of potential revolutionaries and subversives. Before the Second World War Japanese nationals were not allowed to become freemasons (although a few had joined abroad). Taking in a broader picture, at first anti-masonic feeling in Japan was stirred up by the Roman Catholic Church, and this was soon to be linked with anti-semitism through *The Protocols*. Anti-semitic and anti-masonic exhibitions were popular and many were organised by such societies as the *Kokusai Seikei Gakkai* (Society for International Political and Economic Studies) which had the full backing of the Kempeitai.

The attitude in Manchuquo both of the Kempeitai and the Japanese Secret Service towards Jews and Freemasons was summed up in a report by a bureau chief and quoted by Amleto Vespa:

From today henceforth, the Jews, the Masons, and whoever is in sympathy with them [Rotary International and the Boy Scout movement were included] must not be allowed one moment's peace in Manchuquo. Indirectly they must be persecuted, tormented, humiliated without respite. We must make their lives as miserable as possible. We must show those scoundrels that we Japanese can hit back and hit hard. Starting tomorrow [the Kempeitai and Japanese Secret Service] have ordered our two Russian newspapers [*Harbinskoe Vremia* and

Nash Put] to start a merciless campaign against the Jews, the Masonic Lodge, and the YMCA, which is a Jewish–Mason organisation. Rich Jews must be kidnapped daily and made to pay . . . very large amounts. The Masonic Lodge, the YMCA, must be closed. Manchuquo is too good for those dirty rascals. . . .

The leaders of the targeted organisations in Manchuquo showed great courage in the face of Kempeitai persecution. The directors of Harbin YMCA, the US citizens Mr Haag and his wife, were harassed and denounced, with their members physically attacked by the Kempeitai. The Worshipful Master of the Masonic Lodge (UK citizen Mr Neville) was publicly insulted and beaten up, and Dr Kaufmann, President of the Hebrew Association of Manchuquo was similarly assaulted. It was to be a pattern repeated throughout occupied Asia.

At the outbreak of the Second World War Manchuquo was pressured to increase production of minerals to help the Japanese war effort, and Kempeitai activities were taken up with protecting industrial complexes, ports and so on. Assaults on Manchuquo were begun by US bombers in 1944, and on 9 August 1945 Russia invaded. On 18 August, Pu Yi abdicated as emperor. A prominent witness at the International War Crimes Commission at Tokyo, Pu Yi survived five years in a Soviet prison to be handed over to Communist China for 're-education'. He served nine years in prison and lived out the rest of his life as a gardener for the People's Republic and died in 1967. At his abdication Kempeitai activity in Manchuquo was almost at an end.

CHAPTER FOUR

KOREA OF THE KEMPEITAI

As it would be very effective in stamping out the respect and admiration of the Korean people for Britain and America, and also in establishing in them a strong faith in [our] victory, and as the Governor General [Taisho Jiro Minami] and the Army are both strongly desirous of it, we wish you would intern 1000 British and 1000 American prisoners of war in Korea. Kindly give this matter special consideration.

[*Telegram, 4 March 1942, to the* Rikugunsho *from* Taisho *Seishiro Itagaki, Commander of the Chosen Army*]

The appearance of British and American PoWs in Korea was considered of great value in terms of psychological propaganda by the Kempeitai. The significance was expressed by *Taisho* Itagaki in a report to *Chujo* Hideki Tojo, at that time *Gaimudaijin*: 'It is our purpose by interning American and British prisoners of war in Korea to make Koreans realise positively the true might of our empire as well as to contribute to psychological propaganda work for stamping out any ideas of the worship of Europe and America which the greater part of Korea still retains deep down.'

Consequently, the Commander of the 25th Army in Malaya, *Chujo* Tatsumi Kusaba was ordered to hand over White PoWs to the Korean (and Formosan) Armies. The Kempeitai stage-managed a crowd of 120,000 Koreans and 57,000 Japanese to greet the prisoners as they marched through Seoul and Pusan. The poor physical condition of the soldiers, suffering as they were from malnutrition and ill-treatment, added to the impression of a cowed occidental army. The parade was described by an anonymous British soldier who took part in one such march by Allied PoWs:

At about 9 a.m. one thousand British and Australian prisoners of war arrived at Pusan in Southern Korea from Singapore after a journey of five weeks in the Japanese transport *Fukai Maru*. As they disembarked the prisoners were sprayed with disinfectant, photographed by Japanese pressmen and then mustered on the wharf for inspection of kit by the Kempeitai. During the inspection watches, wedding and signet rings and personal photographs were taken by the Kempeitai and never returned to their owners.

After the search, all prisoners, including those who were sick, were made to fall in, in columns of fours, and were marched round the streets of Pusan between the marshalled Korean inhabitants of the city, with the Japanese officer at the head of the column on horseback and Japanese guards on either side. The march went on all day under a hot sun with only two halts in the playgrounds of two schools where the children were allowed to come close up to the prisoners to jeer and spit at them.

The march ended about 5 p.m. at the railway station where each prisoner was given a small oblong fibre box containing cold boiled rice, a piece of dried fish and a few pieces of pickled cucumber. They were allowed to eat this on the platform as it was the first meal they had eaten since 8 a.m. Before entering the train each man was given another similar box of food to last the next twenty-four hours which was to be spent on the train from Pusan to Seoul.

On arrival at Seoul the prisoners were again marched round part of the town before finally entering the prisoner of war camp which

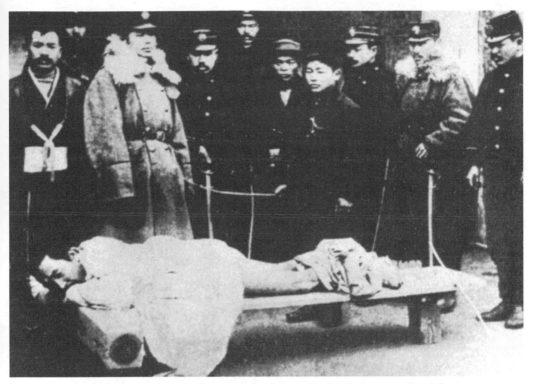

The Kempeitai oversaw the punishment of supposed 'political agitators' in Occupied Territories and extracted 'confessions' by means of torture. Here Korean Kempeitai and civil police stooges interrogate a prisoner in a public spectacle to discourage potential agitators. (JRP)

was to be their home for the next two years. As a result of this propaganda march, and the long train journey on starvation rations, several of the prisoners died a few days after arriving at Seoul.

The success of the public spectacle, the first real attempt by the Kempeitai officially to humiliate the enemy in this way, made the practice common in Japanese–occupied areas.

Korea had come under Chinese suzerainty as early as the T'ang dynasty (618–907), and it became a tributary state of the Ch'ing Empire during 1644–1911. The state had been opened to trade with Japan in 1876, and after the Sino-Japanese War, during which Korea was the cockpit of Japanese aggression, influence steadily grew. During this period a great deal of assistance was given to the Kempeitai by the *Genyosha*, whose subsidiary group, the *Tenyukyo* ('Society of the Celestial Salvation of the Oppressed'), conducted espionage operations to survey the Korean terrain and industrial infrastructure. To pave the way for Japanese continental intervention, the *Genyosha* murdered Queen Min of Korea with the connivance of *Chujo* Saburo Miura, then the Japanese Minister in Seoul. Following the Russo-Japanese War, Japan effectively controlled Korea, 'Land of Morning Calm', and annexed it formally as Chosen on 22 August 1910.

The Japanese set up the *Chosen Sotoku Fu* (Government General of Korea) with the first Governor General *Taisho* Masatake Terauchi. The Japanese colonial government was thus largely military and was the central organ of rule until 15 August 1945. As always the Kempeitai had a strong profile commanded by high-ranking officers like *Shosho* Moto Inkai, who remained commander until the close of 1945, when he was arrested as a suspected war criminal. Terauchi's iron-fisted rule suppressed Korean opinion and political participation. Organised resistance was completely broken by the Imperial Japanese Army with the Kempeitai holding the population in terrorised subservience.

The Korean Kempeitai was to be slightly different in organisation from that devised elsewhere. Out of the initial strictly military police there developed a gendarmerie known as the *Kempei keisatsu*, which operated from 1,642 police stations. In this network large numbers of Korean nationals were employed as assistant Kempeitai. Their brief was to follow through the Japanese policy of complete assimilation for the Korean nation, rather than treating them as residents of an occupied land. With their usual greed, arrogance and brutality the Kempeitai helped exploit the country's resources, which had a ruinous effect on the economy, and carried out the Japanese policy of extirpating the very foundations of national identity, language, customs and a thousand years of culture. Korea was also to be a Kempeitai recruiting ground for 'comfort women' and conscripts to act as PoW guards. As the Japanese held all Koreans in total contempt the Korean camp guards were themselves treated little better than prisoners.

The Korean Kempeitai cooperated with such groups as the *Kokumin Seishin Sodoin Remmei* (League for the Mobilisation of the People's Spirit) which appeared in 1938 to promote total integration into the Japanese way of life. Public thought was controlled and bombarded with propaganda by the Kempeitai through the three daily newspapers, the *Keijo Nippo* (*Seoul Daily*, in Japanese), the *Mai Il Shinbo* (*Daily News*, in Korean) and the English language *Seoul Press*.

Korean will did endure. Following the Versailles Conference, which led to the German Republic signing the Versailles Treaty of 28 June 1919, a group of religious leaders planned a non-violent protest and appeal for independence from the Japanese. Crowds of Koreans began to appear on the streets demanding independence. Caught unawares, the *Kempei keisatsu* panicked and there was a bloody riot. For seven weeks the Imperial Japanese Army and the Kempeitai fought to keep control, with as many as 7,000 recorded killings and 50,000 people injured by clashes and torture. When the riots subsided the *Kempei keisatsu* were replaced by a 'softer' civilian police force working out of the *Keimukyoku* (Police Affairs Department); but the regular Kempeitai remained firmly in place.

In 1937 the policy of complete absorption by Korea of Japanese ways was put into force and the military profile heightened. Soon after the outbreak of the Second World War conscription of all

Korean males over sixteen was enforced, but there were mass desertions. As the war developed, anti-Japanese groups were founded like that of Kim Gu in China and Kim Il-Sung in Manchuquo. They had their successes but throughout the period of the war the Kempeitai controlled the spirit of 'The Land of Morning Calm'.

CHAPTER FIVE

THE SPY RING AND
THE KEMPEITAI

It was brilliant detective work by the Kempeitai which finally broke the Sorge Ring in Japan.

Allan Welsh Dulles (1893–1969)
US Intelligence Overlord

During 1940 and 1941 the Soviet Union was far more concerned with the possibility of a Japanese attack on its eastern empire, from Manchuquo and North China, than it was with the German threat in Europe. Kempeitai files contained a comprehensive dossier on the movements of Soviet spies in the Far East in general, and those within the Soviet News Agency, TASS, in Tokyo, in particular. Soviet espionage had had a poor record in Japan and several failed Soviet intelligence officers, like the military attaché Colonel Rink and Comrade Golkovitch of the *Glavnoye Razvedyvatel'noye Upravleniye* (GRU: Fourth Department of the General Staff of the Red Army), were purged by orders of the Politburo. Thereafter the Soviet Union relied on the machinations of the double agent Richard Sorge. Yet, despite Allan Dulles's praise, the Kempeitai were to be frustrated for a long time by the Sorge case.

Born 4 October 1895 at the town of Adjikend near Baku on the Caspian Sea, the bourgeois idealist Richard Sorge was the child of a

Russian mother from Kiev and a well-to-do German father, a senior petroleum engineer of the Caucuses Oil Company. His family moved to Germany in 1898 and Sorge was to serve in the 3rd Guards Field Artillery Regiment in the First World War and joined what was to become the German Communist Party (KPD) while at the University of Kiel.

Sorge graduated with a doctorate in political science in 1919 from the University of Hamburg. While very active as a communist agent, Sorge became a teacher at Aachen. He was dismissed for his political activism, and became a miner in the Aachen coal fields. Eventually, after attempting to form communist cells at Aachen and in Holland, in 1922 Sorge became an assistant in the social science department of the University of Frankfurt as a front for his communist activity in this the intellectual capital of West Germany. In 1924 Sorge left Moscow, with his wife Christiane, to set up an intelligence bureau for the Comintern and became a member of the CPSU (Communist Party of the Soviet Union). He was to work in Scandinavia, and for a very short time in Britain, on intelligence tasks until 1929, when he returned to Moscow to become a member of the GRU under its director General Jan Karolvich Berzin. Thus his career was to be of interest to both the TOKKO and the Kempeitai; yet, it has to be realised, there was rivalry between the two groups.

At this time there was a major shift in Soviet attention from Europe to the Far East. The Soviets gambled on a successful revolution in China spreading through Asia to destroy the capitalist interests of the European colonial powers and to disrupt the economy of the USA. So in 1929 Sorge was dispatched to the Far East to set up the 'China Unit'. Via Berlin and Paris Sorge travelled to Shanghai on a German passport which described him as a writer. He arrived in January 1930 with a brief to study the social and political structure of the Chiang Kai-shek government and its military strength. He was to pay attention, too, to what he could find out about the China policy of the UK and USA, the strengths and weaknesses of Chinese agriculture and industry and the network of regional groups and factions opposed to the Nanking government. In this data the Kempeitai were far ahead of the Soviets.

The Shanghai of the early 1930s was a Chinese city of overlapping jurisdictions and interests. This main port of the Yangtse Valley was made up of the Chinese City of Shanghai and the International Settlement governed as an extra-territorial international enclave by a Municipal Council elected by the UK, USA, France and Japan. Each policed its own area which was a melting pot of businessmen, artisans and international spies. Among the most active cadre was the Kempeitai.

Sorge made a point of making friends with the new German adviser to the Kuomintang Lt-Col. Hermann von Kriebel, who became Germany's Shanghai Consul-General. Through von Kriebel, Sorge gained useful access to the circles of Chiang Kai-shek's Nanking government and was able to compile a comprehensive dossier on German intentions in China. In due course Sorge urged the Soviets to build up a detailed database on Japanese and German intervention and interests in the Far East, and suggested that he return to Germany, set up a contacts network with leading National Socialists and then return to Japan ostensibly as a friendly member of the German camp. So desperate were the Soviets to thwart any Japanese ambitions against the USSR, that they heeded the womanising, rumbustious, iconoclastic Sorge's suggestions – despite their extreme suspicion of his double-agent credentials. Sorge's work was agreed by Moscow.

Sorge set up what was to be known as the Tokyo Spy Ring, the leading Japanese member of which was Hotsumi Ozaki, the country's greatest pre-war expert on Chinese politics. Although never a member of any communist cell, Ozaki was an intellectual Communist. Born on 1 May 1901, in Shiba (now Minato) Ward,

Tokyo, Ozaki was taken by his family to Japanese-occupied Formosa as a baby; he returned to Japan to be educated during 1919–25 at *Teikoku Daigaku* (Imperial University Tokyo), read law, and subsequently worked as a journalist in Shanghai from 1928 to 1932. In Shanghai Ozaki became involved with Chinese revolutionaries. During 1929–30 Ozaki, as a customer of the *Zeitgeist* bookstore (a branch of the *Zeitgeist Buchhandlung* of Berlin – a Comintern outlet for propaganda), met the left-wing US correspondent for the *Frankfurter Zeitung* Agnes Smedley (1894–1950), a devoted worker for Comintern causes and a keen communist propagandist. In late 1930 Smedley introduced Ozaki to Richard Sorge, describing him as correspondent for the Berlin publication *Soziologische Magazin*, under the name of Mr Johnston.

Because Sorge was anxious to collect data on Japanese intentions in China, Ozaki began in 1930 to assist Sorge to complete this dossier. To help gather intelligence in Manchuquo, Sorge and Ozaki recruited the 29-year-old Teikichi Kawai, a journalist for the *Shanghai Shuho* (*Shanghai Weekly News*). Kawai began to submit his not very helpful reports to Sorge in 1932. The Sorge-Ozaki work was interrupted by the Shanghai Incident.

Fighting had broken out on 28 January 1932 between a Japanese naval landing party and the 19th Chinese National Route Army. The result was that the International Settlement in Shanghai was surrounded by hostile Japanese and consequently the Settlement was in a state of armed readiness with troops of the various powers represented there in a state of high alert. Ozaki was now called to Japan. This was a blow to Sorge, but Ozaki was replaced by Hisao Funakoshi, a thirty-year-old journalist who was soon to be chief of the Tientsin office of Japan's prestige newspaper *Yomiuri Shimbun*. Sorge worked with Funakoshi until he left Shanghai in 1933, returning to Moscow to reassess the future of espionage in the Far East.

In Japan, although factionally divided, the militarists, nationalists and ultra right-wing groups were tightening their grip and

Posters in a Tokyo street for a Kempeitai anti-espionage campaign. They promoted special 'Look-out-for-spies' days to encourage the populace to be vigilant against enemy espionage. (JRP)

influence on Japanese political and public opinion, and assassination attempts abounded. On 9 February 1932 the former *Okura-daijin* (Minister of Finance) Junnosuke Inoue was assassinated by a member of the *Ketsumeidan* (Blood Brotherhood) and on 15 May *Kaigun Heigako* (Naval Academy) cadets assassinated the *Sori-daijin* Tsuyoshi Inukai. TOKKO and Kempeitai arrests became normal daily occurrences, with members of Japan's Communist Party being particular targets.

The Soviet Union was dismayed at the decline of socialist activity in Japan and now stepped up its interest in the country, and a ring of agents was gathered in Japan to assist Sorge's new work. These were Yotoku Miyagi, a Japanese-born member of the US Communist Party and professional artist; Agent 'Bernhardt', a German party worker; and Branko de Vouklitch, a Yugoslav national, Far East correspondent for the Havas Agency of Paris. Sorge arrived at Yokohama on 6 September, having also obtained for himself a German passport and membership of the National Socialist Party. By 1934 the ring was joined by Ozaki, and over the years until their detection there were to be several subordinate members.

Through their journalistic and political contacts ring members now collected data of interest to Moscow, and in 1935 Bernhardt was replaced as radio operator by Sorge's trusted former colleague Max Klausen. From time to time Sorge reported to Moscow in person, with the prime object of keeping his spy masters informed of Japanese foreign policy, particularly if there was any hint of Japan attacking the USSR via North China. Regular briefs were also prepared on Japan's domestic situation and intelligence service. An important contact, too, was to be Gunther Stein, a German-born naturalised British subject who was a prominent left-wing correspondent of such papers as the *News Chronicle*.

Sorge had made a study of the TOKKO and the Kempeitai and was scrupulous in his precautions to avoid the ring's detection. He knew that the Kempeitai interpreted widely the term *gunji himitsu* (military secret) and shadowed all foreigners. So codes were used for all communications and no contact was to be made with either Communists or Russians. The latter decision was a flaw in Sorge's plans which would ultimately cause his downfall.

Between 1934 and 1941, Sorge sent hundreds of reports and rolls of film to Moscow via personal courier and radio transmissions, with important analyses of the nine governments from that of *Sori-daijin* Keisuke Okada to that of Prince Fumimaro Konoye, supplemented with data gleaned from the German Embassy. The

German ambassador, Maj.-Gen. Eugen Ott (who was military attaché in 1934) could not have been more cooperative; he even entrusted Sorge with the task of carrying certain communications from Tokyo to the German Embassy in China. Historians have extrapolated from these events that Sorge's greatest achievement was to uncover the Japanese decision (in the autumn of 1941) to move south against Indo-China, rather than north against the USSR. This knowledge gave Stalin the cue to save Moscow from Hitler's attack, by transferring a large part of the Red Army from the Soviet Far East to Europe.

Sorge's spies worked for eight years without interference from the TOKKO or Kempeitai, or indeed the civil police – a curious occurrence when one realises that the Kempeitai, in particular, was obsessed with *gaijin* activities, however innocent. As responsible government deteriorated in Japan the work of the spy became easier. By 1938 though, the TOKKO already had clues that vital information was exiting the country, for the *Teishinsho* had monitored night-time, illegal radio transmissions from Tokyo to Korea; the Government-General in Korea confirmed this 'cargo'. In 1940 both the TOKKO and Kempeitai were beginning to suspect that a developing espionage network was being built up in Japan, but neither shared information with the other. Yet their advice for the Japanese government was not to step up searches for spies but to tighten the laws on the dissemination of state secrets. Thus the severe *Kokubo Hoan No* (National Defence Security Law) and the *Chian Iji Ho* (Peace Preservation Law) were put in place by 10 March 1941; the punishment for conviction under either was death.

During mid-1940, the Germans began to query Sorge's bona fides as a National Socialist and suspected him of being a double agent for Moscow, even though he had been sending regular and competent reports to Herr von Ritgen, head of the German News Service. So Walter Schellenberg, chief of the foreign section of the *SS Reichssicherheitshauptamt* sent Col. Joseph

Meisinger to Tokyo to investigate. He found that Sorge was held in high regard by Ambassador Ott, yet he informed the Kempeitai that Sorge was under surveillance. The Kempeitai re-opened files they already had on German nationals and now were convinced that the security leaks which they had detected emanated from the German Embassy. The Kempeitai emphasised their belief that Sorge was in fact a double agent spying for both Germany and Russia.

A short while later the TOKKO discovered that the Kempeitai was now investigating Sorge and began to compile its own dossier on him, and came to the same conclusion as the Kempeitai. Sorge was a double agent. The TOKKO intensified their surveillance of Sorge beyond that of the Kempeitai, and arrested his mistress Ishii Hanako. Knowing nothing about Sorge's activities she was unable to incriminate him. Sorge now made the bold move of confronting the chief of the TOKKO Toriizaki police station for frightening a friend of Japan's ally. He received an apology.

Now, too, the TOKKO and Kempeitai commenced an investigation of Hotsumi Ozaki. The Kempeitai wished Ozaki to be arrested for his writings, which they saw as contravening the *Chian Iji Ho*. Thus the Kempeitai office at Akasaka, Tokyo, seized all of Ozaki's writings for analysis hoping to incriminate him as a communist propagandist. Surveillance on Ozaki was also begun by the TOKKO, and they attempted to place a spy, one Ritsu Ito, in Ozaki's office. The TOKKO had arrested Ito some time before as a communist group leader.

With Ito's help the TOKKO built up a picture of a network of communist sympathisers and collaborators. Their list now began to identify, from several sources, Miyagi, Ozaki and Sorge. Miyagi was the first to be arrested for interrogation on 10 October 1941; probably under torture at Tsukiji police station, he revealed data on Ozaki. The TOKKO arrested Ozaki on 15 October. From Ozaki's interrogation the TOKKO obtained the names of Klausen, Vouklitch and Sorge, who was arrested on 18 October.

The main interrogation of the Sorge ring was conducted by the TOKKO, although the Kempeitai made representations that Sorge was a suspect GRU agent and that he and his comrades were military prisoners. The key investigator of the case was Procurator Mitsusada Yoshikawa of the TOKKO Department of the Tokyo District Court Procurator's Bureau. He was no friend of the Kempeitai and endeavoured throughout the investigation to keep them at arm's length.

Sorge did not at first comment on his affiliations with the GRU for he knew from his own researches that he was likely to be executed by the Kempeitai without trial if handed over to them. Ozaki was, however, interviewed by the Kempeitai. A trial was set up in the Tokyo District Criminal Court under the leader of three judges Tadashi Takada. After studying the evidence, the courts gave their verdict on 29 September 1943. '*Hikokuninoshikei ni shosu*' read the verdict, 'the defendant is condemned to death'. Of the ring only Sorge and Ozaki were executed by hanging at Sugamo Prison on 7 November 1944. The naive and trusting German ambassador Ott was declared *persona non grata* and was recalled.

The Kempeitai had wanted to run the whole show in the Sorge trial. Hence, following the arrests the Kempeitai pressured the Military Affairs Bureau of the *Rikugunsho* to complain of TOKKO intervention. A TOKKO procurator was told by Kempeitai HQ in Tokyo: 'We have been sniffing round Sorge's heels; in fact the Kempeitai has been looking into his activities secretly. But in the end we were dished by outsiders.' As the war years went by the Kempeitai were never to be 'dished' again.

CHAPTER SIX

KEMPEITAI MURDER
US AND UK AIRCREWS

It is our duty to detest and loathe the people of the US.

Honorary Chujo *Kennosuke Sato, chief interrogator of*
Allied PoWs, Ofuna Camp, Tokyo

From the first days when mankind undertook war, the treatment of
prisoners of war (PoWs) varied. Over the centuries thousands
of PoWs were slaughtered or sacrificed to pagan gods, enslaved or
ransomed. Christianity did a little to ease the lot of these
unfortunates, but it was not until the eighteenth century that the
concept of feeding, housing and humanely treating PoWs was paid
any more than lip service. During 1785, a Treaty of Friendship was
agreed between the North German state of Prussia and the US,
wherein it was agreed that it was forbidden to retain PoWs in
convict prisons or to manacle them. They had to be fed like
ordinary troops, given adequate exercise and housed in sanitary
accommodation. As the nineteenth century progressed, these
fundamental principles were internationally recognised, and during
15 June to 18 October 1907 the second Peace Conference at the
Hague drew up 'Regulations Respecting the Laws and Customs of
War on Land' in which these principles were made a part of new
agreements.

The Conference resolutions had shortcomings, namely about

conditions in captivity, and the ill-treatment of British PoWs by Kaiser Wilhelm II's Imperial Germany Army during the First World War focused international attention on re-assessing the situation. On 27 July 1929 the representatives of forty-seven states met at Geneva to sign the 'International Convention Relative to the Treatment of Prisoners of War'.

Japan's representative was one of the signatories of the agreement, but the Japanese government had not ratified it when war was declared on 7–8 December 1941. The reason for this was that in 1934 Japan's military authorities strongly opposed ratification believing that such an act would need extensive revision of the strict Japanese Military and Naval Discipline Codes and of the treatment of their own fighting men.

In early 1942, the UK, US and other great powers informed the government of *Sori-daijin* Hideki Tojo that they would abide by the terms of the 1929 Geneva Convention, and requested Japan to reciprocate. Tojo replied that although Japan was not bound by the convention, they would apply it *mutatis mutandis* ('after making the necessary changes') to the PoWs of the UK, US, Canada and New Zealand. Thus he made Japan morally committed to comply with the 1929 provisions in spite of non-ratification. Contrary to Tojo's undertaking, the *Rikugunsho* issued this regulation in 1943: '[If] a prisoner of war is guilty of an act of insubordination, he shall be subject to imprisonment or arrest, and any other measures deemed necessary for the purpose of discipline may be added.' This was to give the Kempeitai *carte blanche* with reference to captured Allied airmen.

The Japanese High Command constantly argued that a ratification of the 1929 Geneva Convention would encourage enemy air raids on the Japanese mainland. They averred that if pilots knew they were to be treated well as PoWs it would increase their range of operations deep into Japanese territory in pursuit of vital supply stores. Enemy bombing of Japan's fire-prone cities was a constant fear of the Japanese government, a terror underlined during the first North American B-25 Mitchells' raid of 18 April 1942 from the carrier USS *Hornet* under the command of flyer Lt.-Col. James Harold Doolittle. The response was for *Sori-daijin* Tojo to order that captured airmen be treated as war criminals and not as PoWs. Hence the death penalty was automatically imposed on enemy airmen captured over Japanese-held territory; he made the order retrospective. The Kempeitai now made treatment and interrogation of US fliers already held in Shanghai and Nanking yet more harsh.

On 28 July 1942 *Taisho* Shunroku Hata, Commander-in-Chief China Expeditionary Army, put on trial the US airmen held in China. Because of their treatment by the Kempeitai the airmen were unfit to plead (or take part in court proceedings) and had no defence representation. They were sentenced to death. Tojo ordered three of the airmen to die, while five sentences were commuted to life imprisonment. The men were executed during October 1942. As a result every airman captured was starved, interrogated, tortured and murdered wherever the Kempeitai held sway. Decapitation was the favoured Kempeitai mode of dispatch. In time the Kempeitai found that formal trials wasted their time, so by May 1945 captured airmen were executed soon after arrest, as long as a dispensation for a court martial had been signed by a district commander.

In China the Kempeitai favoured agonising deaths, which might have enhanced propaganda value if viewed by the populace as a warning. Enemy intelligence would soon relay comment on such executions which the Kempeitai thought would undermine aircrews' morale. In December 1944 at Hangchow (Hangzhou – capital of Zhejiang Province), south-west of Shanghai, three US airmen were arrested by the Kempeitai after being shot down. They were paraded through the streets, ridiculed, beaten and tortured. Again they were forced by the Kempeitai to run the gauntlet of the Chinese peasantry, who taunted them viciously; as they ran they were doused with petrol and burned alive. This time the 'dispensation' for a trial was granted retrospectively to the Kempeitai by the commander of the 34th Japanese Army *Chujo* Senichi Kushibuchi. The parading of prisoners through the streets became a favourite Kempeitai tactic, particularly pilots who had bailed out of B-29s, the feared *Bee ni-ju sikorki* of Japanese parlance.

Another US aviator shot down near Saigon, in Japanese-occupied French Indochina in May 1945, was captured by the Kempeitai in a badly wounded state. He was left untreated for three days then subjected to the usual Kempeitai interrogations. Although transferred to a military hospital, the Kempeitai questioned him daily. The doctors were then ordered by the Kempeitai to 'dispose' of the airman. Army Medical Corps doctors *Shosa* Mabuchi and Nakamura, and *Tai-i* Hisakawa and Nakamatsu were responsible for killing him with Novocaine. At the end of the war all parties were tried by a British military court and sentenced to death by hanging.

During February 1945, an RAF C-87 Liberator crashed in the Pengu district of southern Burma. The crew of six – two flying officers and four flight sergeants – was captured by the Japanese garrison at Pypon and sent to Myanaung on the Irrawaddy River, to be handed over to the Kempeitai who operated from the local civil prison. The RAF officers and NCOs were interrogated in the usual brutal fashion by the Kempeitai, who extracted no information of value. The flight sergeants were then taken 6 miles away from Myanaung into the forest area and interrogated again, to no avail. They were marched a further 5 miles along the road where a group of Japanese soldiers was waiting. The men were lined up on the edge of a trench, blindfolded and decapitated by a Kempeitai officer. The bodies were then used by soldiers for bayonet practice.

The Kempeitai used mental torture as a commonplace, but such military lawyers as Baron Russell of Liverpool cite the Doolittle airmen as recipients of a particular type of mental torture which

A blindfolded US aviator is escorted by Kempeitai personnel to his fate. He is thought to have taken part in (Lt-Gen.) James Doolittle's (1896–1993) B–25 Mitchells raid over Tokyo, 1942. (Random House)

Educated at Pasadena High School, Los Angeles, Gocho Kanai Hiroto, *interpreter for the Kempeitai, interrogated US fliers from the B-24* Taloa *at Hiroshima. (Estate of Kanai Hiroto)*

was revealed in evidence at the International Military Tribunal (on war crimes, 19 January 1946). The time chosen for the mental torture had been sunset. One by one the airmen were blindfolded and marched for a distance and halted. The airmen then heard the sound of a group of soldiers assembling and being drawn up nearby. The clacking of rifles being loaded and aimed was then heard. This action was followed by the voice of a Japanese officer. In his book *Knights of the Bushido* Lord Russell quoted the words allegedly spoken by the officer: 'We are the Knights of Bushido, of the Order of the Rising Sun. We do not execute at sunset but at sunrise.' The airmen were then marched back to prison and told that unless they answered questions fully at the next interrogation they would die at dawn.

On 28 July 1945 a force of B-24 bombers from No. 866 Squadron, 494 Bombardment Group, VII Bomber Command, based at Okinawa, approached Hiroshima. They were on their way back home after their run over Kure naval dockyard – to attack the high-speed Kongo Class battleship *Haruna* – when they came within range of Japanese anti-aircraft guns on Mt. Futaba. Piloted by 1st Lt. Joseph Bubinsky, the first B-24 to come within range was nicknamed *Taloa* and not far behind was 2nd Lt. Thomas Cartwright's *Lonesome Lady*. Standing orders forbade them to bomb Hiroshima City (already 'reserved' for a nuclear bomb attack), so the twenty-three crewmen aboard the B-24s set a course homeward. *Taloa* suffered a direct hit to the nose, and *Lonesome Lady* was also fatally struck, and the crews bailed out. From *Taloa* Joseph Bubinsky, Bombardier Robert Johnston and tailgunner Sgt Julius Molnar drifted to the ground; eight men jumped from *Lonesome Lady*.

From their base at Hiroshima Castle, Kempeitai soldiers fanned out to secure the airmen as prisoners under Kempeitai *Heisocho* Hiroshi Yanagita, and acting interpreter, the US-educated *Gocho* Kanai Hiroto. They soon found Sgt Molnar surrounded by a group of hostile farm labourers. Threatening the mob with instant death if

Gensui *Shunroku Hata (1879–1962) seated third from right with Kempeitai personnel at Hiroshima HQ and officers of the 2nd General Army HQ, Hiroshima, 15 July 1945. Erstwhile senior aide-de-camp to Emperor Hirohito, Hata rubber-stamped Kempeitai actions in Formosa and China during his commands. On Hata's right sits* Chusa Prince RiGi *of the puppet state of Chosen. Far right is* Chusa Oya, *chief of the Japanese US Intelligence Section, who interrogated Kempeitai-held airmen at Hiroshima Castle Prison. He denied resorting to torture, and 'forgot' responsibility for the murder of PoWs at Fukuoka, Kyushu. Oya was known to be alive in the 1970s and was a frequent visitor to the USA. (Estate of Kakuzo Oya)*

they did not disperse, the Kempeitai arrested the sergeant. Initial on-the-spot interrogation revealed only age, rank, number and unit; Molnar said that he did not know the name of his fellow crewmen nor how many had jumped. He was joined by US bombardier Robert Johnston who had been arrested nearby. Along with pilot Joseph Bubinsky and three other crewmen the US airmen were taken to Hiroshima Castle. In all, fifteen crewmen of the two bombers survived to enter Kempeitai captivity.

The US fliers were put into individual cells at three different locations around Hiroshima. Their cells were sparcely furnished and their food was indifferent. They were regularly interrogated by the Kempeitai and subjected to continual jeering by their guards. Some of the airmen were to invent stories about their war service and told the Kempeitai what they thought they wanted to hear. This only prolonged their suffering.

The fliers remained in captivity until 6 August 1945, when at 8.16 a.m. nuclear destruction rained on Hiroshima from the bomb doors of the B-29 dubbed *Enola Gay*. Records show that most of the airmen died in the nuclear bomb raid. Anecdotal evidence notes that two may have been clubbed to death in the grounds of Hiroshima Castle by the Kempeitai, while two others were stoned to death by Japanese civilians. Pilot Cartwright had been taken to Tokyo for further interrogation by the Kempeitai so was saved, while his tailgunner Wilbur Abel had avoided arrest and had hidden in the hills around Hiroshima. He gave himself up to the Kempeitai on 7 August 1945 and although severely tortured, he was one of the few captured Allied airmen to survive the war.

CHAPTER SEVEN

KEMPEITAI VERSUS THE BRITISH LION

[Do not look upon my Kempeitai] with fear and suspicion as a kind of secret police force. This is most distressing. You need not fear them. [Kempeitai measures are] inevitable to bring us to victory in the Dai Toa Sen.

Shosho *Hakujiro Kato, Commander of North China Special Unit, and concurrently Commander of North China Expeditionary Force Kempeitai*

The first Englishman to set foot in Japan was William Adams from Gillingham, Kent. Known as *Miura Anjin* (Pilot of Miura) by the Japanese he had arrived in Japan in 1600 as pilot-major of the Dutch vessel *Leifde*, the sole survivor of a squadron of merchant ships that had set out from Amsterdam for the Far East in 1590. After a period of imprisonment, having been denounced as pirates by Jesuit agitators who had the ear of the *Shogun*, Adams and his compatriots were allowed to settle in Japan. In due time a 'factory' was set up at Hirado to develop English trade and through this the foundation of Britain's contacts with Japan were established. The factory, however, was to close when the 45-year-old Adams died in 1620 and Anglo-Japanese contacts were not properly revived until the Japanese Restoration period of 1868. At this time Sir Harry Parkes (1828–85) became the first British Minister to Japan, a post he was to hold for eighteen years.

Despite a few incidents which occurred during the troubled times of the Restoration period, until just before the outbreak of the Second World War Japan and Britain enjoyed years of cordial relations. In 1902 this relationship became the basis of the Anglo-Japanese Alliance, and in 1921 the Crown Prince of Japan (later Emperor Hirohito) paid a visit to Britain.

Britons played an important role in the development of modern Japan, particularly in organising the Imperial Japanese Navy and in the evolution of the railway system, and the Japanese looked upon British industry as the fount of twentieth-century craftsmanship. Yet there is something in the Japanese psyche that can turn respect and admiration into a paranoid hatred when a former friend makes them 'lose face'. Thus the British were to encounter much odium at the hands of the Kempeitai.

During 1937–41 Sir Robert Leslie Craigie (1883–1959) was UK Ambassador Extraordinary and Plenipotentiary to the *Dai Nippon Teikoku*. A career diplomat, Craigie had served as Assistant Under-Secretary of State at the Foreign Office from 1934 and was well versed in diplomatic affairs. Even so, he had little direct experience of Far Eastern affairs and was given one of the most difficult diplomatic jobs of the era. From his initial arrival in Japan aboard the Canadian Pacific liner *Empress of Russia*, he was well aware that his activities, and those of his staff, were monitored by the Kempeitai, who also discouraged British subjects from visiting the *Eikoku Taishikan* (British Embassy) regularly. As John Morris put it in *Traveller from Tokyo* (1943): '. . . after Japan entered the war a number of our nationals was arrested for the 'offence' of having paid regular visits to their own embassy. The [Kempeitai] were unwilling to believe that one might go there with no more dangerous object than to drink a cup of tea.' Yet, in the international diplomatic circles of pre-Second World War Japan, embassy surveillance by the Kempeitai was treated at worst as an irritant and at best as a farce.

Sir Robert (Leslie) Craigie (1883–1959), and Pleasant, Lady Craigie, with members of the British Embassy Staff, during internment, 8 December 1941 to 30 July 1942. Craigie was British Ambassador to Japan, 1937–41 and during 1945–8 was UK Representative to the UN War Crimes Commission. (JRP)

Wartime SOE agent Ronald Seth recalled diplomats' amusement at the Kempeitai obsession with the movements of Dr Walter Donath, Chief of the German Cultural Institute. On one oft-recounted occasion Donath made a journey to a branch of the Institute on Shikoku Island along with a Japanese student as interpreter. From ticket booking hall to ferry and beyond, Donath was regularly accosted by Kempeitai agents asking fatuous questions about his business, his antecedents and his opinion about the Japanese. Each time he paused he observed the

Kempeitai agents stop and scribble vigorously in a notebook. Each of Donath's visits to the bathroom and each meal taken were religiously recorded. Despite these ludicrous antics, many British internees on being interrogated on arrest were astounded at the detailed files the Kempeitai had on them. One journalist marvelled at the fact that the Kempeitai had photocopies of 'every letter she had written and received over a period of several years'.

Craigie was not subjected to such severe surveillance as Donath, yet he was moved to insist that known Kempeitai withdraw from meetings if he was conducting government business. Craigie found it easier, too, to meet Japanese 'on an informal footing' at his house at Hayama, a seaside resort some fifty minutes from Tokyo. Nevertheless the Kempeitai watched the house. Later the Rt Revd Samuel Heaslett (1875–1947), Bishop of South Tokyo, and the most senior Anglican clergyman in Japan, recognised one of the Hayama Kempeitai as 'one of the most brutal of his inquisitors . . . after the outbreak of war'; the bishop had been arrested on no legitimate charge and was incarcerated for four months.

Among scores of innocent UK nationals who became embroiled with the Kempeitai, Craigie was concerned with two in particular, Jimmy Cox and Sir Vere Redman. From the early days of 1941 Kempeitai paranoia concerning the 'espionage activities' of all Japan-based foreigners increased to a zenith on the acceptance of the Imperial Mandate to form a government on 17 October by their champion Hideki Tojo. Anti-British propaganda in particular in which, as Lewis Bush described in his *Land of the Dragonfly* (1959), posters 'warning of sinister foreigners shown dressed in Sherlock Holmes rigout with curly pipe and deerstalker hat' had led to the arrest of eleven prominent UK civilians including Cox.

Melville James 'Jimmy' Cox, Reuters correspondent in Tokyo, was a forty-year-old married man who had adopted two Japanese

British Ambassador Sir Robert Craigie with (left) Gensui Shunroku Hata, C.-in-C. of the 2nd General Army, and (later Gensui) Count Hisaichi Terauchi (1879–1946). As Supreme Commander of all army invasions, campaigns and activities in Occupied Territories, Terauchi agreed to Kempeitai programmes from Indo-China to New Guinea. Records aver he ordered the Kempeitai (and other army personnel) to kill all PoWs in the Southern Occupied Territories should the US Forces invade mainland Japan. (JRP)

orphans. He was popular among the foreign correspondents who regularly met in the journalistic haunts of Tokyo, like the America Club. Cox was arrested on 27 July 1940 by the Kempeitai on the usual non-specific charge of espionage. Cox had for some time, though, been making himself a nuisance at *Gaimusho* press briefings. He asked a barrage of awkward questions and made no effort to cover up his contempt and growing animosity for the Japanese militaristic state. After he entered the brownstone headquarters of the Kempeitai near the unrippled green moat and granite walls of the *Kyujo* (Imperial Palace), he was never seen alive again by any foreigner. Two days after his arrest, Cox was seen falling from an open window on to the concrete courtyard of Kempeitai headquarters. It was not the first time the Kempeitai had alleged that a victim had leapt to his or her death.

There had been no violence, noted a Kempeitai officer at the press conference held concerning the case. It was not common practice for the Kempeitai to explain their actions to anyone, but the international ramifications of the Cox case brought them out of the sewer. They produced an unsigned letter from Cox to his wife which they alleged had been found in his pocket. The Kempeitai spokesman insisted that they had irrefutable evidence – which was not produced – of his 'espionage guilt'. 'What of the hypodermic marks visible on his body?' asked one correspondent. Just injections of medical fluids used to try to revive his unconscious body in the courtyard, hissed the Kempeitai officer. No one was convinced.

The British Embassy was sent a copy of the statement on the death of Cox issued by Yakichiro Suma of the *Gaimusho*. It read:

According to a joint announcement by the *Rikugunsho* and *Homusho*, Melville James Cox, Reuters correspondent in Tokyo, one of those arrested on a charge of espionage, threw himself from a third-storey room of the Tokyo Kempeitai headquarters on July 28 at 2.05 pm in an attempt to commit suicide, although the guards tried to stop him. He died at 3.46 pm.

A note addressed to his wife was discovered on his person which read as follows:

See Reuters re rents.

See Cowley re deeds and insurance.

See Hgk Bank re balance and shares in London. [i.e. the Hongkong and Shanghai Banking Co.]

I know what is best

Always my only love

I have been quite well treated

But there is no doubt how matters are going.

In the light of the above note, it seems that, with the progress of the investigation, the deceased became aware of the fact that he could not escape conviction of his crime. [NB: This is the exact form and style in which the unsigned note was set out in the official report.]

Largely because of the reputation of the Kempeitai, the received opinion of foreigners in Japan was that Cox had been so badly harmed by drugs and beatings – the usual Kempeitai inducements to 'voluntary' confessions – that the only option to mask the damage to his body was to throw him from an upstairs window. Because Jimmy Cox was so well known in the international community the Kempeitai could not just have him vanish, as others did; they needed to produce a body. Even if it was suicide, the incident was an acute embarrassment for the Kempeitai, for the arrest of Cox and others formed a propaganda move to show how they had uncovered and broken a 'spy ring'. The mercurial *Gaimu-daijin* Yosuke Matsuoka issued a report exonerating the Kempeitai, but some months later he informed the British Embassy that Mrs Cox (who had been sheltered by the embassy after the event and had been repatriated to Canada) was to be given 'a substantial exgratia payment'. The Cox's adopted children vanished.

The case of Vere Redman and the Kempeitai followed the declaration of war. At 8.30 a.m. on 8 December 1941, the telephone wires to the British Embassy were severed by the Kempeitai. By this time, though, Ambassador Craigie had ordered the destruction of confidential archives and cyphers and had recalled members of staff who lived outside the diplomatic compound. Following Craigie's return to the embassy from a hurried meeting at the American Embassy to compare notes with US ambassador Joseph Clark Grew, the embassy gates were closed from the outside. The embassy was now visited by Ichiro Ohta, head of the British Section of the *Gaimusho's* western European Division, demanding to impound the 'radio transmitter'. The British Embassy had never had one, but the Kempeitai removed all other wireless sets. Craigie's staff were now informed that they were officially interned until 'evacuation became possible'.

Herbert Vere Redman (1900–75) was then Head of the Information Department of the British Embassy and produced the news sheet which it issued to counter German propaganda. Although the irascible, eccentric Redman did not publish anti-Japanese statements, he was on the Kempeitai hit list as a supposed spy and at the behest of the National Socialist regime. As with all foreigners in Japan who dealt in information, Redman was thought of as a spy by the Kempeitai, largely because the Japanese word *joho* (information) also means intelligence.

On the day of his arrest Redman had made his way to the British Embassy as usual, so when the Kempeitai arrived at his Tokyo lodgings to arrest him, he had already left. They seized his French wife Madeline as a hostage to ensure his surrender and made for the British Embassy. Ambassador Craigie had already been warned by the Argentine Chargé d'Affaires Señor Villa (the Argentine Embassy undertook to represent British interests after the declaration of war) that the Kempeitai were to arrest Redman. The intention had also been spelled out to Craigie by Yoshitane Kiuchi, Chief of the Protocol Department of the *Gaimusho*. By this time the Kempeitai had released Mrs Redman because of diplomatic pressure and the Redmans were both inside the embassy when 'sixty plain-clothes' armed Kempeitai under a *Kempeitai Taisa* came to effect the arrest.

Craigie refused to give up Redman to the Kempeitai and he was taken by force, one Kempeitai officer inflicting a minor assault on the ambassador. It was a clear breach of diplomatic privilege by the Kempeitai. The embassy arranged to supply Redman with food during his captivity and with the insulin needed to suppress his diabetes. In fact it was later learned that the Kempeitai withheld the insulin in an effort to make him confess. Yet for weeks all news about Redman's fate was censored by the Kempeitai. In all he was subjected to over 800 hours of humiliating interrogation during eight months' solitary confinement at Sugamo prison, a detention prison in the suburbs of Tokyo where most foreigners arrested in the city were incarcerated.

At first the Kempeitai charged Redman with 'collecting and sending abroad information detrimental to the interests of the Japanese empire'. This they altered to 'conspiring to prevent the execution of Japanese national policy'. The direction of interrogation in this matter showed how the Kempeitai was involved in international politics, for the change indicated that they believed Redman was playing a role in separating Japan from Germany following the Tripartite Alliance of 1940.

After his period of sustained interrogation Redman was tried before a district court in Tokyo. To his complete astonishment and that of his colleagues he was acquitted and returned to the British compound. Meanwhile the Redman case had been the subject of reprisal; in London a member of the Japanese Embassy staff, Kaoru Matsumoto, was arrested to ensure Redman's repatriation.

The usual embassy 'family' of twenty now swelled to sixty as the Kempeitai ring closed around the British compound. Obtaining supplies of food and fuel to sustain the comfort of that number was always a problem, but somehow the embassy was able to send a portion of their rations to the British internment camp in Tokyo. During the spring of 1942 British interests were to be handled by the Swiss Legation as all South American missions to Japan had been repatriated. Swiss Minister Camille Gorge now had regular contact with the British, and his colleagues in occupied China were also dealing with British Kempeitai internees in places like Shanghai.

The Japanese government decided to evacuate the British Embassy staff on 30 July 1942 with those from the British consular offices at Yokohama and Kobe. Although they were escorted by Misayoshi Kokitsubo, a representative of the *Gaimusho*, the Kempeitai made the journey to Yokohama as bureacratic and as uncomfortable as possible, forcing the staff to carry their own luggage whatever their state of health. As Ambassador Craigie commented, '[it was] a petty effort to humiliate officials of the United Nations in the eyes of Japanese spectators'.

At first the British were locked below decks of the 400-berth vessel *Tatsuta Maru* in the searing heat of Yokohama harbour; at length they were allowed on deck for exercise but only behind screening from the dockside. The voyage of repatriation was to last ten weeks, the ship sailing to Lourenço Marques, Mozambique, dodging German U-boats. The journey was via Singapore and *en route* the group was joined by other repatriates from Kempeitai jails in Shanghai and Saigon. With the group travelled the *Gaimusho* representative *Danshaku* Yasushi Hayashi; Craigie asked him to enquire about the state of British nationals in prison camps in Singapore. The Commander-in-Chief at Singapore, *Taisho* Tomoyuki Yamashita would not allow Hayashi to land but sent a staff officer with vague but positive reports of the prisoners' welfare and promises of regular Red Cross parcel distribution. Craigie could hardly realise the horrific reality of the prison situation on Singapore. At last from Lourenço Marques the repatriates boarded the SS *El Nil* and the SS *Narkunda* and returned to Liverpool. In the Far East thousands of British soldiers and civilians were to endure three more years of Kempeitai cruelty.

CHAPTER EIGHT

LEGIONS OF THE DAMNED

Dear friends, pardon us. . . . But we have suffered heavy casualties. So just pardon us . . . have you any last wish before we kill you?

Extract from the address given before Chujo *Akira Naka ordered the slaughter of PoWs at Pantingan River, Philippines*

From the jungles of the old kingdom of Siam to the building sites of Singapore, the bones of Kempeitai *furyo* (PoWs) and victims are regularly disinterred by the activities of modern agriculture and construction. No one knows for sure how many PoWs – civilian and military – were murdered by the Kempeitai in the Second World War 'Killing Fields' of the Far East, for even the 'official graves' records tell no individual stories of Kempeitai infamy.

Ten kilometres from the centre of the city of Hodogaya, on the Yuenchi-Dori road which forks left off the medieval Tokaido highway from Tokyo, lies the Yokohama War Cemetery. Constructed by the Australian War Graves Group, the cemetery has a section each for the war dead of the UK, Australia, Canada and New Zealand, with a plot for the Indian Forces. Three Crosses of Sacrifice stand over 1,518 classified graves and the memorial urn with the ashes of 335 soldiers, sailors and airmen of the UK, US and Netherlands, who died as PoWs. A large proportion of them, and many a 'not identified' cadaver lying here, are reckoned to have been slaughtered by the Kempeitai and their auxiliaries.

As the events of the Second World War unfolded the most extreme horrors of the Kempeitai were to occur in the PoW and civilian internment *furyo shuyojo* (camps). Today the archives of the Allied wartime nations contain flesh-creeping testimony of the condition of these camps. Prisoners were kept in their own filth and squalor in overcrowded pens with totally inadequate food and water. Disease-ridden, starved and exhausted these legions of the damned, beyond all reach of justice, were made to work day and night with regular beatings for flagging or rebellion.

Article 6 within an annex of the Hague Convention of 1907 (ratified by Japan) noted that it was not illegal to put PoWs to work for pay. The Geneva Convention of 1929 (not ratified by Japan) extended this Article, and in 1942 the Japanese government guaranteed PoW wages. Yet what the Articles forbade was for PoWs to work on projects to aid war. The Kempeitai deliberately procured PoWs, both military and civilian, impressing them into slave labour gangs for war work. They recruited both Allied PoWs and conquered native peoples to work for such arms companies as Mitsubishi Heavy Industries whose wartime board of directors maintained direct links with the Kempeitai.

Within the PoW camps the Kempeitai made great efforts to devise tortures of the most depraved kind in an attempt to 'speed up' their success rates of cooperation. First-person accounts show clearly that Kempeitai tortures went far beyond the infliction of pain to extract information, or as punishment for defying the rules of the Sons of Heaven.

Forcing prisoners to stand for days on end crammed inside tight cages set on top of vicious red ants' nests, or lashing dehydrated prisoners with barbed wire to the trunk of a tree and without water for days, while captors regularly guzzled from a bucket of fresh water in front of them, were among the milder of Kempeitai infamies.

119

KEMPEITAI

In the course of the Second World War the Japanese incarcerated in excess of 140,000 White Allied prisoners out of a total of 350,000 prisoners taken. It was these White Caucasians who suffered consistently at the hands of the Kempeitai. The Japanese had captured some 180,000 Asian troops, too, from Filipinos serving with the Americans to Indians fighting alongside the British. Most of the Asians who managed to survive the brutal initial months of captivity were released, as were the vast majority of non-Japanese ethnic oriental service personnel. This was part of the Japanese propaganda drive to act as 'liberators' of the Far East. An exception were those of Chinese extraction; the age-old Sino-Japanese mutual contempt, and Japanese hatred of Chinese influence in the Far East, lay behind the Kempeitai acts of genocide against the Chinese.

Almost all Japan's PoWs were taken within the first months of the war. PoWs, of whom 27 per cent died in captivity, were housed in 176 camps in Japan's home islands and in 500 camps in the Occupied Territories from the Burma/India border to New Guinea. When the Japanese judged an occupied area to be ready to join their *Dai Toa Kyozonken*, the area army chief would 'abolish' the military administration and hand it over to a collaborating civil authority. This helped them 'legitimise' their grip over the territory within which they imposed a puppet administrator. In reality nothing changed. For instance in Burma the Japanese selected one Dr Ba Maw as 'Prime Minister', but real administrative influence emanated from *Taishi* Ranzo Sawada and *Shosho* Buryo Isomura, Deputy Chief of Staff to the Japanese Burma Area Army. Thus the Army and the Kempeitai kept control of the PoW (work) camps in Burma and monitored what they perceived as subversive elements 'working against the Burmese people'.

In the Occupied Territories many of the PoW camps were near native villages. By and large the locals would shun the Kempeitai whether in the street or on public transport, yet many

Taisho *Shojiro Iida, Commander of the Imperial Japanese 15th Army (under Burma Area Army),
inaugurated a new puppet government on 1 August 1942 in Burma under the lawyer Dr Ba Maw
(1893–1977). A phoney independence was granted to Burma by the Japanese in 1943 with Ba
Maw as* adipati *(Head of State). On Japan's defeat, Ba Maw fled to Japan and was later to serve
an Allied prison sentence. His position in Burma assured by the Kempeitai, here Ba Maw poses
wearing the Japanese decoration of 'Order of the Rising Sun with Paulownia Leaves'. (JRP)*

Japanese Occupation banknote for Malaya: pale green, One Cent with M=Malai. Centre-bottom calligraphy reads 'Japanese Government'. Some Kempeitai officers operated and condoned scams in counterfeit notes. (JRP)

villagers risked Kempeitai retribution by dealing with PoWs. Some natives traded for altruistic motives and others through pure greed. The Kempeitai often turned a blind eye to such trading as many a military policeman had a private scam with the locals.

By March 1942 an office was set up by the *Rikugunsho* for the administration of PoWs. The office was to oversee the handling of PoWs in the three areas of occupied territory. Section One of the administration office controlled prisoners in Japan, China, Korea, Manchuquo, Formosa and the Philippines, along with the territories known as the *Nan 'yo-cho* (the Southern Region). Section Two dealt with the Imperial Army-controlled territories of the Celebes, Borneo, the Moluccas, Timor, the Lesser Sundas, New Guinea, Rabaul, the Bismarck Archipelago, Guam and Wake.

Within their jurisdiction, too, lay the Imperial Navy control area of the *Tokei-tai*.

While all other territories were covered by Section Three, the Army's areas extended from Burma to the Dutch East Indies. *Taisho* Hideki Tojo ensured that all camp commandants knew that they must expunge all effete western ideas of humanitarianism and for PoWs to be handled strictly, with the Kempeitai having access at all times to the daily running of the camps.

Tojo himself laid down rules for camp administration, but all on-the-spot regulations were left to camp commanders to interpret. Most of the time camp activity depended upon the whims of the alcoholic, the sadistic, the disaffected and the homicidal senior officers who ran so many of them. Colloquially the Kempeitai would refer to camps as the personal fiefdom of the commandants, dubbing them, for example, *Taisa Nakamura Butai* ('Camp Colonel Nakamura'). Camps were run on Tokyo time, irrespective of time zones, so *tenko* (roll calls) and work party duties often took place during hours of darkness.

Although it violated the Geneva Convention, Japanese camp commanders made prisoners agree to sign non-escape oaths. Those who refused to sign, and those who attempted to escape and were subsequently re-captured, were made examples of by being beaten and tortured in public spectacles. In truth it was the duty for UK, US and Australian soldiers to try to escape, and often senior officers ordered their men to sign the oaths to avoid retribution; it was understood that such signatures meant nothing. The Kempeitai were unable to comprehend this apparently blatant disobeying of orders and the command went out that for every PoW escaping ten comrades should be beheaded.

The Japanese adopted the spectacular horror of execution by decapitation, by the by, from the Chinese, although the *Kojiki* ('Record of Ancient Things', the earliest source book in Japanese literature and history, completed in 712) illustrates it as a noble retribution, and the skilled ultimate suicide for the *samurai*, which long pre-dated *harakiri*. (See: Glossary under *seppuku*.) For the Kempeitai the act of beheading assured a trophy from an enemy vanquished, a trophy that would be displayed as a warning to others. To the Kempeitai there was nothing more didactic and salutary to a group of recalcitrant PoWs than a public beheading. Kempeitai officers regularly practised their decapitation skills (on live and inanimate objects) so that they could remove the head with a single stroke of their regulation army sabres.

Two types of Kempeitai were to be encountered by PoWs. The Field Kempeitai, who served only in wartime, were top-flight officers who were as likely to appear in civilian dress as in uniform. They worked closely with the *Tokumu Kaikan*, and were mostly recruited for service in Occupied Territories from the ranks of those who had worked for a long time in Asian countries prior to the war. Regular Kempeitai made up the second group.

PoWs suffered much at the hands both of Korean nationals who served in the camps as well as of the lower echelons of the Kempeitai. The Japanese camp guards treated their Korean counterparts hardly better than they did the PoWs. The Koreans had the rank of *kanshi-hei*, lower than a *nitohei*. In the camps the Koreans wreaked bloody vengeance on the unfortunate PoWs for the thirty years the Japanese had run their homeland as a military colony. Most of the Korean Kempeitai were trained in the Manchu Military Academy in Manchuquo and had been treated severely by their Japanese instructors; this harshness also led to their brutality in their work in the camps.

Kempeitai charge books were full of references to their being called to 'incidents' by the camp commanders. The definition of 'incident' was very widely interpreted by the Kempeitai and could range from the trivial to obvious breaches of security. Private Roy H. Whitecross of the Australian 8th DIV AIF reported in his *Slaves of the Son of Heaven* (1952) how the camp commandant of River Valley Road Camp 17, near Omuta, Kyushu, one *Tai-i* Fukuhara, was informed that a US PoW called Hubbard had been caught with a 'torn scrap of a Japanese newspaper'. Fukuhara summoned the Kempeitai. 'If Hubbard had been found carrying a bomb,' wrote Whitecross, 'the Japanese could not have made more fuss. He was bashed by the entire guard and thrown into the *aeso* [Japanese guard house]. Next day three Kempeitai corporals came to the camp. They beat Hubbard . . . with their rifle butts. Four days Hubbard's screams echoed across the subdued camp – until merciful death claimed him at last.'

The Kempeitai were the administrators of Japanese military law in occupied territories and operated two extant types of court martial. The trial of members of the armed forces according to laid down military law (cf. western courts martial) was called *gumpo kaigi* whereas *gunritsu kaigi* was the trial of civilians by military court. At the beginning of the Second World War the Kempeitai went through the motions of these procedures, but as the war went against Japan the Kempeitai favoured the *tokubetsu gumpo kaigi* (special court martial), at which the defendant was permitted no legal representation and no right of appeal.

One camp 'incident' investigated by the Kempeitai which led to a court martial appeared in their archives as the famous 'Sandakan Incident' which took place in the Allied PoW camp at Sandakan on the north-east coast of Borneo Island. The camp was within the remit of overall PoW camp commander *Taisa* Tatsuji Suga, in whose name the Kempeitai carried out their investigation under *Heisocho* Seisaku Murakami. Sandakan housed some 2,500 Australian and British PoWs by September 1943, six of whom survived until 1945. Here the camp guards were all impressed and resentful Formosans under Kempeitai supervision.

Contrary to international law, prisoners at Sandakan were put to work on military airfield and service road construction. As part of their opposition to the enforced work the PoW camp leader

Captain Lionel Matthews had selected some twenty officers and NCOs to form an intelligence group within the camp. Using trusted native intermediaries Matthews's group managed to make contact with British civilians being held on nearby Bahara Island and a network of information was exchanged on Japanese troop movements, Kempeitai strength and main areas of presence. They also found out that a few civilians – mostly doctors and dentists – were being allowed by the Japanese to move freely in the local township. Through Dr J.P. Taylor, the PoWs were able to obtain medical supplies, information about the surrounding villages and their terrain and about where the Japanese strengths and weaknesses were. The clandestine supplies were also to extend to parts of a radio receiver.

The Kempeitai high command were obsessed with radios and transmitters, or PoWs obtaining any news about the war at all. Regularly groups of PoWs would be rounded up for interrogation in an attempt to find any clues as to whether radios were being built or used. Kempeitai interrogation followed a set pattern. Serious questions were mixed with the banal. Queries about a PoW's ancestry, life before the war, and such questions as 'Who will win the war?' were all part of the Kempeitai interrogator's handbook. Why did *furyo* wish to listen to foreign broadcasts, when Japanese radio stations told the truth? Matthews and his fellow PoWs soon found out from the regular questioning that the Kempeitai interrogators knew nothing about the details of radio construction and the dangerous work continued.

The Sandakan radio receiver was duly constructed and was powered illicitly by a camp generator. In this way BBC and US broadcasts were picked up and a weekly news bulletin was successfully circulated. The more news its members heard that Japan's war machine was crumbling at the advance of the Allies, the more emboldened did Matthews's group become, and searches were made in the local township for guns and ammunition to secrete in the camp to be used to help with the recapture of Borneo. A cache was hidden by the PoWs (who managed to carry out their hush–hush duties while on work tasks outside the camp) near the town of Sandakan. The group now decided to build a radio transmitter and went about obtaining the vital elements of the system from the sympathetic Chinese civilians with whom they had already made contact. Alas, one of the Chinese, one Joe Ming, allowed himself to be observed helping the PoWs with their 'shopping list' and was betrayed to the Kempeitai (after an unsuccessful blackmail attempt) by an Indian co-worker.

The Kempeitai arrested Joe Ming, the 'collaborator of the *furyo*', and tortured him and his family until they had the names of those involved in the radio transmitter plan. All the members of the Matthews group and their civilian contacts outside the camp were arrested. The Kempeitai thoroughly searched the camp and discovered a list of parts from which the radio was made. A sustained three-month programme of interrogation and torture at the Kempeitai HQ at Kuching, where the PoWs and the collaborators had been moved, broke down the radio conspirators and the Kempeitai closed the 'Sandakan Incident' file with *seiko* (favourable termination). Matthews and eight of the ringleaders were executed.

The Kempeitai were just as brutal in the civilian internment camps as they were in the camps for war combatants. One of the greatest concentrations of civilian prisoners was in Sumatra where around 13,000, mostly Dutch, civilians were housed in gender-segregated camps; children were usually interned in the women's camps. At one of these camps at Brastagi, North Sumatra, the Kempeitai were called in to deal with a break-out by the women internees. The prisoners' leaders at the camp Mevrouw Prins and Mevrouw Eikens had petitioned the camp commandant for increased rations because of the escalation in cases of malnutrition. Although the commandant promised to look into the matter, no action was taken and on 27 November 1944, 386 women broke out of the camp. The Kempeitai were called and the women were rounded up and returned to the camp.

All the internees' leaders were arrested by the Kempeitai and interrogated with the usual brutality. One leader, a hospital nurse Verpleegster Schuddeboum, was cruelly beaten with a curtain rod. On hearing her screams Mevrouw Prins protested to the Kempeitai *kashikan* in charge and was told that tough questioning would stop when all the prisoners' leaders confessed to their guilt as rabble rousers and encouragers of women to break out of the camp. Mevrouw Prins left this record of what happened next:

> I retorted sharply that the Japanese were themselves guilty, which so enraged the Kempeitai NCO that he struck me with the same curtain rod, on my back, shoulders and neck about six times and with such force that it broke in two.
>
> That evening I was summoned again for questioning, but I sent a message that I was unable to walk and could not come. The following morning I was ordered to attend at the commandant's office with the other camp leader and six other women.
>
> On arrival we were all driven to the penitentiary at Katon Djahl, where, on our arrival, our coats and hairpins, if any, were taken from us and we were locked up. Mrs Eikens and I were each thrown into a small cell and the six other women were put together in a larger one. My cell was without light or ventilation, the floor was wet with urine, and excreta were smeared all over the walls. I learnt later that these cells were used to house lunatics who were *en route* for the asylum. There was no bed in the cell and no lavatory receptacle.
>
> I remained there all night, and in the morning was taken by the warder to a room in an outbuilding at the rear of the prison.

Two members of the Kempeitai were there. I saw lying on a table a selection of weapons, cudgels, belts and whips and in the centre of the floor a lighted brazier with irons heating in it. I realized that I was in the torture chamber, although very little light came in through the small window.

I was then put through the same interrogation as before. Pointing to the instruments, one of the Kempeitai threatened me with torture unless I pleaded guilty. When he found that I refused to do so he made me stand on a chair, after he had tied my wrists tightly together behind my back. He tied a rope, which ran over a pulley right over my head, to the cord around my wrists and pulled the other end until I could hardly reach the seat of the chair with the points of my toes . . . he kept on raising and lowering me until my arms were nearly pulled out of their sockets. Each time he lowered me he said, 'Do you plead guilty?' to which I replied, '*Nippon salah*' ['The Japanese are wrong'], and each time I gave that answer he beat me on my back with a rubber truncheon. After about ten minutes I said to him, 'White officers do not behave like this,' and he suddenly let go of the rope and the sudden jerk caused me excruciating pain, and my nose started to bleed profusely.

Two Indonesian policemen were then called in to take me back to my cell. They helped me along, and showed clearly that they disapproved of my ill-treatment and were sorry for me. When I reached my cell door, however, the Japanese warder pushed me into the cell with such force that I fell flat on my face on the filthy floor and lay there for a long time completely stunned.

Later Mevrouw Prins was taken back to the Kempeitai torture room and the same procedure was repeated. When the sordid performance had ended the most senior of the Kempeitai staff present entered the room and asked if she had changed her opinion about Japanese officers. She indicated that she had not and he slapped her face. Again she refused to name the women who had led the exodus from the camp. Next morning she was informed that she and Mevrouw Eikens had been condemned to death. At the War Crimes Trials at Tokyo she gave this testimony as to what happened then:

> About one hour later Mevrouw Eikens, Mevrouw ten Bloemendaal and myself were taken to a large room where we expected to be shot. We were placed with our faces to the wall and our hands crossed behind our backs. . . . We then heard some Japanese soldiers enter the room behind us and heard the noise of rifle bolts being opened and closed. Another Japanese entered the room and gave a word of command in a loud voice which we thought was the order to fire. We waited for the end to come but nothing happened. Mevrouw ten Bloemendaal could not control her curiosity and peeped behind her. 'They cannot fire, because the dust covers are still on their rifles,' she whispered. The Japanese officer gave a second command, whereupon we were struck once by one of the soldiers, and led out of the room.

From time to time the Kempeitai used PoWs in investigations concerning their fellow soldiers. One such case involved Erik Leeuwenburg of the Netherlands East Indies Army who acted as *tsuyaku* at the Tamarkam camp situated by the native village of Thanbyuzayat where the Imperial Japanese Army had established an HQ for the construction of the Rangoon-Bangkok railroad. The case in which he was involved concerned *Chusa* Yoshitada Nagamoto, Chief of No. 3 Branch of the Thai War Prison Camps, Thanbyuzayat, and was being conducted by *Tai-i* Nagoya of the Kempeitai.

Leeuwenburg was terror-stricken when he was arrested for no reason by the Kempeitai and taken to Kanchanaburi Kempeitai

HQ. For three days he was kept locked up with six Dutch prisoners, not knowing what was to be done with him, yet conscious of the terrible tortures going on in the compound around him. Sometimes the screams of the tortured hardly sounded human; it was a part of the Kempeitai softening up process of people whom they wished to use.

On the fourth day of his captivity a Kempeitai *kashikan* came to take him to the HQ building. Here he met *Tai-i* Nagoya. To Leeuwenburg's relief and no little bewilderment Nagoya began his interrogation with '*Ima no hanashi wa dare nimo zettai ni hanasu na*' ('What will be discussed here must never be told to anyone.') He went on to detail accusations of malfeasance by *Chusa* Nagamoto. It was to be one of the most curious interviews ever conducted by a Kempeitai officer. Nagamoto in truth was ripe for war crimes execution. He had been responsible for the slaughter of over 1,000 PoWs through overwork and cruelty and had buried their bodies in the Burmese mud along the railway route. Yet here was Nagamoto being accused of 'inhuman treatment' of fellow Japanese. To top the list of accusations Nagamoto was accused of insulting the emperor by speaking English.

What Nagoya wanted was a written list from Leeuwenburg of every occasion on which he had had dealings with Nagamoto, and the latter's association with the PoW leaders of the camp. It was clear to the Dutchman that Nagamoto was being accused by a fellow officer to discredit him for personal reasons. For three days Leeuwenburg was interrogated concerning Nagamoto with the gnawing fear that at the end of it all he too would be disposed of. On the threat of severe beatings Leeuwenburg signed dispositions against Nagamoto hardly understanding fully what he had signed. Two days later he was released.

PoWs of European stock attempting to escape from Japanese prison camps were faced with two almost insurmountable difficulties. The harsh terrain of the colossal landmass of Japanese-occupied Asia made progress on foot slow and painful.

Secondly, no white-skinned escapee could ever hope to blend in with the dark-skinned, short-statured natives. Yet assistance was given in escape – how to survive the jungles and deserts and evade the Kempeitai net – by the MI (Military Intelligence) department MI–9 (cf. US Department MIS–X), founded on 23 December 1939 and with headquarters in Room 424 of the Metropole Hotel, Northumberland Avenue, London, under the direction of Maj. Norman R. Crockatt. MI–9's advance base in the Far East was at New Delhi. Code-lettered GSI(e) – E Group after 1943 – it had been set up in October 1941 by Lt-Col. Robin Ridgway.

In the Chinese provinces of Kwangtung (abutting Hong Kong) and neighbouring Kwangsi, BAAG (British Army Aid Group) – MI–9's independently operating group under Lt-Col. (Sir) Leslie Ride – had success in gathering intelligence and aiding those escaping from the Japanese. An important part of BAAG's work, too, was to strengthen morale in the PoW camps, clandestinely supply necessary materials, medicines and food for the PoW ill and starving and advise on escape techniques. BAAG also assessed the strength and ruthlessness of the local Kempeitai commanders; it was important to ascertain if the Kempeitai would set in motion reprisals for any successful escapes and, if so, how to limit the retribution. Further BAAG plotted the positions of PoW camps in respect of Kempeitai HQ to assess if they could be knocked out from the air before escapes might be made. Often ammunition dumps were sited abutting the camps.

BAAG's work was made more difficult by such as the anti-British chief of Chiang Kai-shek's (China's nominal ruler at Chungking) secret service, General Tai Li, and the fact that no fewer than six separate secret police forces including the Kempeitai were working in Southern China. BAAG's rescue teams picked up most of the UK's Air Force evaders being searched for by the Kempeitai, and thirty-eight US airmen who had crash-landed near Hong Kong were rescued, as well as PoWs in the Hong Kong camps of Argyle Street and Sham Shiu-po. Lt-Col. Ride's 'rat lines' also rescued many civilians in the Hong Kong–South China areas who were useful to the British Crown and who had been targeted by the Kempeitai. BAAG further breached Kempeitai security by evacuating Chinese dockyard artificers, thus rendering Hong Kong's dockyard of little value to the Japanese.

E-Group devised a code of practice for Allied personnel captured by the Kempeitai. In essence it went like this. Fundamental Rule: 'Your duty on capture is to avoid being a source of information and to escape if the opportunity arises.' Demeanour: 'Be patient, courteous, and respectful. Firmly decline to give information beyond Name, Rank and Number. Emphasise to Kempeitai interrogators that to give more would be against Military Codes of Practice. Do not act superior, or try to deceive, but try to appeal to the Japanese codes of chivalry. Use flattery. Do not cringe, but play dumb, as many junior Kempeitai interrogators and auxiliaries are dumb.'

The British SOE (Special Operations Executive) also had a hand in thwarting the Kempeitai within the Occupied Territories and played a part in the rescue and succour of PoWs. In particular, Colin Hercules Mackenzie's Force 136 (the Far East arm of the SOE) operated some 3,000 spies, saboteurs, assassins, propagandists and guerrillas (along with 30,000 auxiliaries) countering many a Kempeitai programme all over Asia.

CHAPTER NINE

AFTERMATH

O, the joys and worries of life are gone and with them I fade too. Yearning for my mother and father.

Tai-i *Sato of the 3rd Field Kempeitai, Java, on receiving a death sentence for war crimes*

Senso owari – at last the war was over. On 15 August 1945 at 1200 hrs, from Studio 8 of *Nihon Hoso Kyokai*, Tokyo, Emperor Hirohito's recorded voice broadcast his famous surrender speech to the Japanese nation. Only his voice, the *Koe no Tsusu*, the sacred 'Voice of the Crane', could bring Japan to heel. Only his command could outweigh all the opposition to surrender from high-ranking commanders within the Imperial Japanese Army and the Kempeitai.

At Kempeitai HQ, Kudan, Tokyo, *Chujo* Sanji Okido, overall commander of the Kempeitai, had announced the country's impending surrender and the emperor's broadcast to his senior officers himself. He had already been warned by *Rikugun-daijin Taisho* Korechika Anami that he should only listen to orders that came from the *Rikugunsho*, for it was likely that a coup would be attempted by disaffected army officers to prevent a surrender taking place.

The Kempeitai were to be involved in shadowing potential rebels. From the army bomb shelter at the *Rikugunsho* on Ichigaya Hill, Tokyo, a group of officers under *Chujo* Masahiko Takeshita were planning to assassinate those who had advised surrender. Elsewhere youth movements were being stirred up to oppose surrender. At Atsugi Air Base young pilots were being harangued by the mentally deranged Navy *Taisa* Yasura Kozono to become impromptu *kamikaze* against all the emperor's enemies. In the event there was no mass rebellion against surrender, only a series of ritual *seppuku* to expunge the Emperor's name from the guilt of losing the war.

From the Imperial Japanese Army HQ at Tokyo orders had been sent to all Kempeitai commanders in the field when the surrender had been confirmed. They were to disperse and vanish. Many officers did just that, but other ranks in such places as Java were in prison, themselves to be tortured by their new masters, and, incredibly, in the Indies former Kempeitai soldiers helped the Allies keep the peace among the Indonesian nationalists. For at least two weeks after the surrender Kempeitai and PoW camp commanders continued the slaughter of the defenceless. To tidy up their records at Ranau, Borneo, the Japanese authorities murdered their thirty surviving PoWs. Those PoWs who emerged from the camps elsewhere were now RAMPs – Recovered Allied Military Personnel, and were at last free from the ministrations of the Kempeitai.

As the days of peace numbered into double figures, stories of Kempeitai infamy all over the Occupied Territories emerged to pile up in a horrific mass indictment. Torture, mass murder, bacterial warfare experiments, cannibalism, genocide . . . the files against the Kempeitai towered in every Allied commander's office. How were those accused of *Senso Hanzai* (war crimes) to be brought to justice? All was to be dealt with through the commands of one man.

Douglas MacArthur (1880–1964), Supreme Commander for the Allied Powers (SCAP), Commander-in-Chief Far East (CINCFE) and Commanding General, US Army, Far East, landed at Atsugi Airfield, Kanagawa, on 30 August 1945, aboard the plane *Bataan*, on the runway used a few days previously for *kamikaze* missions. MacArthur was to take up immediate duties as commander of the

During November 1945, 131 officers and other ranks of the Saigon-Cholan Kempeitai were assembled under an escort of the 23rd Indian Mountain Regiment, Royal Indian Army, to surrender at Chi Hoa. Here the surrendering officer bows to the Union Jack and the Subedar-Major of the Surrender Ceremony. He presented his sword as a token of surrender, and shortly afterwards Maj.-Gen. Douglas D. Gracey, General Officer Commanding 20th Indian Division, presented it to a female member of the French Resistance. (Stuart A. Guild)

forces of occupation in Japan and his Central Administration Offices were centred on the Dai-Ichi Building, the Goodwood Park Hotel and the Meiji Building, Tokyo. MacArthur remained in charge until April 1951 when he was replaced by General Matthew Ridgway, who headed the occupying forces until the official treaty of peace between Japan and its erstwhile enemies of April 1952.

The occupation of Japan was 'Allied' on behalf of thirteen nations, but only US personnel served as an occupying force. The administration occupation proper began on 4 January 1946 with the first 'purge' of certain high-ranking Japanese politicians such as *Sori-daijin* Kijiro Shidehara's (1872–1951) cabinet; and as a token gesture to equality Shidehara was shorn of his title *Danshaku*. A first major task was for MacArthur to accept the *Nihon Kofuku Bunsho* (Japan's official surrender) on 2 September 1945 aboard the battleship USS *Missouri* anchored in Tokyo Bay. There *Gaimu-daijin* Mamoru Shigemitsu and *Taisho* Yoshijiro Umesu signed for the defeated Japan. On 1 November 1945 MacArthur disbanded the then 36,000–strong Kempeitai and his staff got down to the matter of supposed war criminals.

The *Kyokuto Kokusai Gunji Saiban* (International Military Tribunals for the Far East) were drawn up by MacArthur. Records of the trials are fragmentary and scattered and no systematic study was published. There were three classes of war criminal. Those in Class A were deemed policymakers who had conspired to wage aggressive war. These accused appeared at the Tokyo Trial, the equivalent of the German Nuremberg Trials (20 November 1945 to 1 October 1946). Classes B and C were those who ordered atrocities, condoned their carrying out or actually took part in them. These accused were tried by the Allies in the areas where the crimes had been committed. In all, around 5,700 trials of B and C Class criminals took place, with 3,000 convictions and 920 executions. One historian averred that this was one execution for every 250 Allied PoWs murdered.

These tribunals were conducted in Japanese and English, and the

Led by a Kempeitai officer (who has surrendered his sword and belt) and still wearing their armband insignia, men of the Saigon-Cholan Kempeitai march off to jail. (Stuart A. Guild)

Tokyo Trials in the auditorium of the *Rikugunsho* were convened under the court president, Australian Sir William Webb. Eleven nations were represented at the commencement of the trials on 3 May 1946 and the proceedings ended on 4 November 1948, when judgments were made. The most famous trial was that of the former *Sori-daijin* Hideki Tojo within the trial of twenty-eight Class A defendants who had been selected by the Allies from scores of

A survivor of Kalagon village, north of Moulmein, Burma, picks out members of the Kempeitai at an identity parade at Moulmein Jail. During July 1945 the Kempeitai had taken part in the massacre of 637 Indian villagers. The identifier was one of five survivors. (Hulton Getty Picture Collection)

wartime military and civilian leaders. Of the twenty-eight two died in captivity; these were former *Gaimu-daijin* Yosuke Matsuoka and *Taisho* Osami Nagano, erstwhile Chief of the Naval General Staff; the policy-maker and promoter of the *Dai Toa Kyozonken* Shumei Okawa (1886–1957) was deemed too insane to be charged. The twenty-five Class A war criminals remaining can be identified thus:

Name	Sentence	Erstwhile Position	Known/Suspected Kempeitai Connection
Sadeo Araki (1877–1966)	LI	*Rikugun-daijin*	Through Inspectorate of Military Training
Kenji Doihara (*b.* 1883)	E	*Taisho*	Army Intelligence/ Manchuquo campaign
Kingaro Hashimoto (1890–1957)	LI	*Chusa*	Imperial Rule Alliance/Secret Society
Shunroku Hata (1879–1962)	LI	*Rikugun-daijin*	Hiroshima Castle Kempeitai
Kuchiro Hiranuma (1867–1952)	LI	*Taisho/Sori-daijin*	Not known
Koki Hirota (*b.* 1878)	E	*Sori-daijin*	Resident-General, Korea, 1905
Naoki Hoshino (1892–1975)	LI (Released 1955)		Manchuquo/Secretary-General to Tojo
Seishiro Itagaki (*b.* 1884)	E	*Taisho*	Manchuquo/Singapore
Okinori Kaya (1889–1977)	LI (Released 1955)		Rikugunsho
Koichi Kido (1889–1977)	LI (Released 1953)		Tojo's cabinet
Heitaro Kimura (*b.* 1888)	E	*Chujo*	C-in-C Burma
Kuniaki Koiso (1880–1950)	LI		Governor-General, Korea
Iwane Matsui (*b.* 1886)	E	*Taisho*	C-in-C, Shanghai 'Butcher of Nanking'

Name	Sentence	Erstwhile Position	Known/Suspected Kempeitai Connection
Jiro Minami (1874–1957)	LI		Governor-General Korea Ambassador to Manchuquo
Akira Muto (b. 1892)	E	*Chujo*	Ex-chief Military Affairs Bureau
Takasumi Oka (1890–1973)	LI (Released 1954)		Ex-chief Navy Affairs Bureau
Hiroshi Oshima (1886–1975)	LI (Released 1955)		Ambassador to Germany Pro-National Socialist
Kenryo Sato (1885–1975)	LI (Released 1956)	*Chujo*	Ex-chief Military Affairs Bureau, Army Command, Siam
Mamoru Shigemitsu (1887–1957)	7 years	*Gaimu-daijin*	Not known
Shigetaro Shimada (1883–1976)	LI Served 7 years	*Taisho/Kaigun-daijin*	Not known
Toshio Shiratori (1887–1949)	LI	Ambassador to Italy	Pro-National Socialist
Teiichi Suzuki (1888–alive 1983)	LI (Released 1956)	*Chujo*	Possible association while advisor Chinese puppet government, Nanking
Shigenori Togo (1882–1950)	20 years	*Gaimu-daijin*	Not known
Hideki Tojo (b. 1884)	E	*Sori-daijin*	'Father of the Kempeitai'
Yoshijiro Umezu (1882–1949)	LI	*Taisho*	Chief of General Staff

KEY: LI - Life Imprisonment   E - Execution 1948
Although some entries bear the comment 'Not known', all the above condoned in some way the actions of the Kempeitai. All other war criminals were released in 1958.

Emperor Hirohito (1901–88) reviews his troops while riding his famous Imperial Grey.
Considered a god in his pre-surrender days, it was in the name of the Emperor that all
Kempeitai activities took place. (JRP)

Emperor Hirohito, in whose name the Kempeitai had acted, was given absolution from prosecution as a war criminal through a provision of the Initial Post Surrender Policy by MacArthur. During the Tokyo trials Emperor Pu Yi, Japan's former puppet ruler of Manchuquo, was summoned as a witness; it was proposed by the Soviet representative to the Allied Council, Lt-Gen. Kuzma N. Derevyanko that Hirohito also be called to appear. Because of the 'absolution', the suggestion was strongly opposed by MacArthur and the US Chief Prosecutor Joseph Kennan 'in the best interests of the Allied powers'. As Shigeru

Yoshida, *Sori-daijin* 1946–47, 1949–55, said in his *Memoirs* (1961): '[MacArthur] had come to have a great respect for the Emperor, and even told me once that, although Japan had lost the war, the Throne was still important to the Japanese people and the reconstruction of Japan depended upon the people rallying to the Imperial symbol.'

More controversial in the minds of many was the 'blanket absolution' of members of the imperial family. Many were dismayed that Hirohito's uncle *Chujo* Prince Yasuhiko Asaka, who had ordered the Imperial Japanese Army and the Kempeitai to slaughter 300,000 military prisoners at Nanking (for which *Taisho* Matsui paid the capital price), should go free, along with another uncle Prince Naruhiko Higashikuni who had ordered the bombing of civilians in China. Then there was Empress Nagako's great-uncle *Gensui* Prince Kotohito Kanin, member of the Supreme War Cabinet and a senior adviser to Hirohito, who was said to be a strong supporter of the Kempeitai. And, worst of all in some eyes, *Chujo* Prince Kuni, Hirohito's father-in-law, who had spearheaded the Manchuquo Germ Warfare Centre (Unit 731).

Nevertheless, during the period of the War Crimes Trials the Civil Censorship Department of the US Occupation Forces, under the Chief of Counter Intelligence, pursued a rigid censorship of newspapers, radio scripts, films, plays, records, books, magazines, pamphlets and *kamishibai* (paper picture-card shows for children) to expunge any justification of Japan's war effort or of the war criminals.

Along with the twenty-five Class A war criminals interned at the now demolished Sugamo Prison, Tokyo, were a number of minor Kempeitai officers. Something of their final moments can be pieced together from the records of the late Shinsho Hanayama, Buddhist chaplain to the prison, extracts from whose papers appeared in the *Asahi Shimbun* in the late 1940s. Hanayama's records show the lack of remorse among the Kempeitai even in the face of impending death. Some of these men like *Chu-i* Sadamu Motokawa of the Tokyo Kempeitai 'devoted' their last days to religion. Motokawa gave this last poem to Hanayama: 'Wandering now through field and now in mountain/How far must a pitiable traveller continue his journey?/May he not stray, but find a way to the awakening.' The 'awakening' was a new life in the pantheon of the *kami* as a god.

Allied executioners endeavoured to silence the triumphalism of some of the Kempeitai, who, as they stood hooded to be hanged shouted the traditional triple *Banzai* or *Tenno Banzai*. As one hangman put it: 'I tried to release the drop before the bastards got out their last *Banzai.*'

The Kempeitai cruelties of the occupation years in such theatres of war as the Philippines have never been forgotten. On the fall of Japan the collective rage of the inhabitants of the Occupied Territories was only one aspect of reaction, with captured Kempeitai being pelted with stones as they marched to captivity. The US authorities in Manila had countless applications for the job of hangman as the *Philippine Free Press* newspaper was to record.

In the Philippines the fate of captured Kempeitai (as with other Japanese Army personnel) was determined by the War Crimes Division of the US Judge Advocate's Office, Manila, and US military commissions to examine cases were in place by December 1945. Each commission of military personnel with experience of the law was directly appointed by Douglas MacArthur.

A huge amount of eyewitness accounts and documentation against the Kempeitai was available to the commissions. The first trial of a Kempeitai officer was that of *Chusa* Seichi Ohta, on 27 December 1945. Dubbed 'The Ogre of Fort Santiago', Ohta had been Commander-in-Chief of the Kempeitai in the Philippines. He was specifically charged with 'ordering his subordinates to inflict torture and kill Chinese consulate staff'. Ohta testified on his own behalf and denied all charges. He averred

Tried as a Class A War Criminal at Manila, and executed by firing squad at Los Banos, Luzon, on 3 April 1946, Chujo Masaharu Homma, Commander of the Imperial Japanese 14th Army (South Expeditionary Army), allowed the Kempeitai a free rein in the Philippines. Held responsible for the 'Bataan Death March', Homma was a pro-British protégé of Emperor Hirohito's brother Prince Chichibu. Homma had served as an observer with the British 2nd Army HQ in France during the First World War and was awarded the British Military Cross. (JRP)

that he had forbidden torture and only allowed 'light force' during investigations. He pleaded higher orders for the killing of the consular staff. The evidence against him was overwhelming and he was found guilty and sentenced to death by hanging on 13 February 1946.

More than forty-seven prosecution witnesses testified against Ohta's second in command *Tai-i* Akira Nagahama. He refused to defend himself or deny the horrific charges of torture, murder and mass maltreatment. He believed the policy he had enacted had been right to control the 'hostile Filipinos'. Found guilty, he was sentenced to death on 11 March 1946. Other officers tried were quite open about the terror they had inflicted. *Shosa* Shimpei Harada, Chief of the Cavite Detachment Kempeitai, averred: 'While I was the commander . . . my duty was . . . to destroy the guerrilla members. I had to order my men to [torture and kill].' He was condemned to die by 'musketry'. The Philippines military commissions tried some twenty-four Kempeitai officers and civilian interpreters. Sentences ranging from death to imprisonment with hard labour were handed out; *Sho-i* Junzo Matsuta was the first Kempeitai officer to be acquitted of wrongdoing.

For a period of years afterwards Kempeitai personnel and Filipino collaborators were sought out for trial. In 1952 President Elpidio Quirino of the Philippines conditionally pardoned all the remaining Japanese war criminals in the Philippines with the proviso that they 'will leave the Philippines for Japan'. Anti-Kempeitai feeling did not abate and assaults on the pardoned Kempeitai were not unusual. In an act of incredible insensitivity former Kempeitai officer Fumio Fujihara turned up at the Philippine Embassy in Tokyo with a gift of a Christmas tree. He was recognised by some of the staff as an erstwhile Kempeitai and was beaten by staff members until he vomited blood. Fujihara was one of the former Kempeitai who eventually returned to the Philippines and in the 1960s became head of the Fujisa Trading Corporation.

Tens of thousands of former Kempeitai personnel escaped retribution. Many took on new identities, some throwing away their paybooks and assuming the persona of private soldiers killed or missing in action. When the war had begun to go against the Japanese, Kempeitai officers' records were tampered with by the Imperial Japanese Army Records Section staff, and Kempeitai muster rolls were deliberately 'edited' to list personnel as being transferred to other duties. The Japanese high command were anticipating post-war crimes trials.

There were a number of reasons why the subsequent trial evidence against Kempeitai officers was slow in being compiled, and why some known officers were never brought to trial. The Japanese administrators helping the War Trials Commissions deliberately operated delaying tactics. Investigations, too, were hampered by British military bureaucracy. Local Japanese precinct police were thus given time to alert Kempeitai agents in hiding if their pursuers were getting too near and many former Kempeitai personnel were shielded by the *yakusa*, a part of the 'underground network' whose job it was to keep war criminals two steps ahead of arrest.

In current Japanese the word *yakusa* means gambler, gangster, or just good-for-nothing. They are the Japanese equivalent of the Mafia. By the Second World War the *yakusa* had a deep and well-established historical background. As early as the fourteenth century Japan's gangsters had flourishing cadres, openly flouting the authority of the feudal administration. A civil protection group grew in the 1850s and 1860s which constituted the roots of the modern *yakusa*. Its role was largely self-defensive.

Yakusa activites fitted well with the personal ambitions of the Kempeitai, particularly of those officers who had trained and served in Manchuquo. Just as the *yakusa* were unethical, so were many Kempeitai, and ex-Kempeitai officers became 'lost' in the complicated *gumi* (families) of the *yakusa*. Because the *yakusa* had their own links with big business, and some big companies were to act as money launderers for the *yakusa*, it was easy for *yakusa* to insinuate former Kempeitai into employment within post-war Japanese companies.

A huge blow to the cause of bringing prominent Kempeitai officers to trial was suffered with the sudden death – some say murder – of Colonel Cyril Hew Dalrymple Wild. Himself a PoW, Wild was a fluent Japanese speaker and had been interpreter for Lt-Gen. Arthur Percival, commander of the Singapore garrison. He was an investigator of war crimes issues for South East Asia Command and personally interviewed such war criminals as *Chujo* Tomoyuki Yamashita, 'Hero of the Siege of Singapore'. Wild was to give evidence at the International Military Tribunal at Tokyo and put together a comprehensive set of files on well-placed Japanese who were perverting trial evidence. Yet, if the murder conspiracy historians are to be believed, it was the fact that Wild insisted on a report being made on Emperor Hirohito's war career, and on the activities of the Kempeitai, that spelled out his own doom. On 25 September 1946 Wild had boarded a two-engined Dakota at Hong Kong's Kai Tak airfield en route for Singapore. With him he had a briefcase of incriminating documents on the Kempeitai and, some say, on the emperor. A few minutes into the flight, after the Dakota had passed over Kowloon, the plane for no apparent reason nose-dived from 4,000 ft to crash on the hillside. All aboard were killed, and all the documentation was destroyed. In that briefcase, too, correspondents were told, had been files on one potentially convicted war criminal who was never brought to justice but who had stage-managed one of the most notorious instances of Kempeitai genocide ever. The scenario was Singapore.

From around 1923 the Japanese had begun extensive espionage in Malaya, within both civilian and military areas, and by 1936 had a formidable intelligence service operating in the Malay Peninsula from Singara (Siam) in the north to Johore Bahru in the south. Within the service were Kempeitai agents. The pacifist views of

James Ramsay MacDonald's Labour cabinets of 1924 and 1929 had thwarted the construction of a naval base at Singapore from preliminary work in 1924, and only in 1934 was work properly begun. This was despite Japan's threatening influence in the whole South China Sea area since 1919. The whole defence system at Singapore was not completed until 1939.

On 23 September 1940 the Japanese entered northern Indochina, and by April 1941 the Japanese government had forced the French to allow them access for their troops and to build an airfield in their territory. By 10 December the Imperial Japanese Army was well into Malaya and at sea the battleship HMS *Prince of Wales* and the old inadequately armed HMS *Repulse*, of the Z Force Squadron, were sunk by bombers of the Japanese 22nd Air Flotilla. The Royal Navy were thus humiliated in an ocean they had controlled for 200 years. During 8–9 February 1942, the Japanese attacked Singapore.

At 5.15 p.m. on Sunday, 15 February 1942, the British under their commander Lt-Gen. Arthur E. Percival surrendered Singapore to the invading Japanese 25th Army of *Taisho* Tomoyuki 'Tiger of Malaya' Yamashita, in a cramped office of the Ford factory, Bukit Timah Road. Emperor Hirohito now re-named Singapore *Shonan*, 'The Radiant South'. The first Japanese military into Singapore City ahead of the main force of *Shosho* Saburo Kawamura's 5th Division 9th Infantry Battalion was a specially formed garrison force known as *keibitai*, a mixture of Kempeitai and *Hojo Kempeitai* (auxiliary military police) of the 2nd Field Kempeitai. The first Kempeitai HQ was set up at Tonjong Pagar police station under *Tai-i* Hisamatsu.

Five days after the surrender the Japanese began the systematic *shukusei* (purge) of Singapore's Chinese civilians. Their target was 50,000 executions in an endeavour to eliminate all opposition to Japanese rule. To this end Singapore was divided into 'screening areas' to identify and contain the purported 'anti-Japanese elements' for eventual 'disposal'. The soldier behind this screening and

Tableau at the recently restored 22-room Battle Box, Fort Canning Hill, recreating the action just before the surrender of Singapore by Lt-Gen. Arthur Percival, GOC Malaya. Fort Canning became the HQ of Shosho Saburo Kawamura, commander of the conquering Singapore Garrison Army. The Kempeitai were sent in ahead of the main force to conduct a programme of genocide against Singapore Chinese. (Fort Canning Country Club Investment Ltd)

execution programme was the fanatical arch-militarist *Chusa* Masanobu Tsuji, Chief of Planning and Operations, and the screening was mostly conducted by the Kempeitai who also carried out the subsequent executions. Because of the enormity of the task units such as the Konoye Imperial Guards under *Chujo* Tokumo Nishimura were called in to assist.

Chusa Tsuji was to manipulate the indecisive *Shosho* Saburo Kawamura, Singapore Garrison Commander, in his own holocaust solution to the 'Chinese problem'. Towards this end Kawamura, assisted by *Shosa* Tadahiko Hayashi, a creature of Tsuji's, liaised with *Chusa* Masayuki Oishi of the No. 2 Field Kempeitai at the temporary HQ at the Singapore Supreme Court.

In time the Singaporeans began to identify places to avoid. There was the Cathay Building – ex-British-Malay Broadcasting Corporation – home of the Japanese Propaganda Department; and the Kempeitai 'torture houses' of the old YMCA building (East Branch Kempeitai), Orchard Road; Singapore Improvement Trust shophouses (now demolished; modern New Bridge Centre), New Bridge Road; Smith Street (Western Branch Kempeitai); South Bridge Road Centre police station, and Oxley Road HQ. The main Kempeitai registration centre was at Sook Ching, Hong Lim Complex, and murdered body dumps were at Changi Beach, Ponggol Foreshore and Serapong Golf Course, Sentosa. The *Tokei-tai* operated from a building which houses the present St Andrews Mission Hospital, Tanjong Pagar Road, under Naval *Tai-i* Nagai and *Sho-i* Hinomoto.

Chusa Oishi quickly and meticulously divided Singapore into manageable sub-divisions under *Shosa* Tomotatsu Iyo and *Chusa* Yoshitaka Yokota, who commanded the screening of all civilians and categorised Chinese suspects as 'undesirable and anti-Japanese'; and decided who should die. Soon Kempeitai lock-ups were bulging with suspects, and during 17–24 February 1942, the Kempeitai executed 700 Chinese from this lock-up alone. *Chusa* Tsuji monitored every step of the killing programme, berating the Kempeitai if the numbers of Chinese slaughtered seemed to fall. In all some 5,000 persons were to be murdered in Singapore in the 'Tsuji holocaust'. Imperial Japanese Army HQ in Tokyo monitored Kempeitai activity in Singapore through their liaison officer, the former Kyoto Kempeitai and ex-Manchuquo 'old hand' *Taisa* Kenjiro Otani. He took up duties at Singapore on 6 March 1942

YMCA Building, Stamford Road, Singapore, HQ of the Singapore Branch Malay Kempeitai of the 4th Branch Kempeitai, Southern Army. This is probably the most notorious Kempeitai interrogation and torture centre of the Second World War. Here the Kempeitai held prisoners in five vermin-infested underground 'cages', with lights permanently on and with no room to lie down in comfort. From 8 a.m. to 10 p.m. inmates were forced to sit bolt upright in rows on the bare floor squatting Japanese fashion. Any movement resulted in a beating. (William Hodge)

and stayed for eighteen months. Otani's subsequent records showed that what was begun as a *shukusei* developed into a *bogyaku* (tyranny) on the scale of Kempeitai atrocities on the Chinese mainland.

On 7 September 1945, the British War Office ordered all Kempeitai personnel and their associates to be seized and held to

Former civilian residence at the corner of New Bridge Road and Smith Street, Singapore, used by the Kempeitai as a jail. This was the scene of many Kempeitai atrocities. Another Kempeitai prison was located at Outram Road. (William Hodge)

answer war crimes charges. This directive came three weeks after Britain's land forces in South East Asia High Command had asked for orders concerning suspected war criminals. On 23 February *Taisho* Yamashita was executed by hanging at Los Banos, Laguna, Philippines as the chief war criminal. But the man who had organised the Kempeitai round up, *Chusa* Masanobu Tsuji, was to escape the Singapore War Crimes Section. A further seven men were to be tried for what was called the 'Chinese Massacre' following Yamashita's death; among them were the Singapore Kempeitai supremo *Chusa* Masayuki Oishi and his aides *Chusa* Yoshitaka Yokota, *Shosa* Tomotatsu Iyo, *Shosa* Satoru Onishi and *Tai-i* Haruji Hisamatsu and the two *chujo* Nishimura and Kawamura. Their trials were duly undertaken and Kawamura and Oishi were condemned to death by hanging while Nishimura, Yokota, Iyo, Onishi and Hisamatsu were sentenced to life imprisonment.

The Chinese community was not satisfied with the trials' outcome and demanded the death sentence for all seven. In the event the sentences stood. Kawamura and Oishi were hanged at Changi Jail where so many Kempeitai horrors had begun. Five years later Nishimura was tried by the Australian authorities for slaughtering Australian and Indian prisoners and on being found guilty was hanged on 11 June 1951. Yokota, Iyo, Onishi and Hisamatsu were repatriated to Japan in 1950.

During July 1942, *Chusa* Masanobu Tsuji had been recalled to Tokyo, and was to serve in China and Burma where he continued his killing programme. In Burma he ordered the execution of the downed pilot Lt Benjamin A. Parker of the 14th USAF 25th Flight Squadron, 51st Fighter Group. Military historian James Mackay reported that Tsuji ordered a portion of Parker's flesh to be cut from his dead body and later had it cooked to be served to the officers' mess.

As an arch–militarist Tsuji was opposed to Japan's surrender as set out in the Potsdam Demands of the Allies. Several senior officers like him believed that the Nationalist Chinese Kuomintang would be the leaders of East Asia, so a switch of allegiance to support them in their fight against the communists seemed a sensible move. In the meantime, though, Tsuji would have to 'disappear' to avoid being arraigned for war crimes. So he disguised himself as a Buddhist monk and joined other military fanatics at the Ryab Temple, Bangkok which had had links with Japanese Buddhists. On 16 August 1945, Tsuji wrote a false will and a fake suicide note.

From his hiding place he now set out to make contact with the Kuomintang.

By this time British forces had entered Bangkok, but Tsuji, disguised as a Chinese businessman, managed to escape with the help of the Kuomintang network. Via Indochina and Hanoi he flew to Chungking and arrived there on 9 March 1946. Tsuji began to work for the Anti-Communist Propaganda Department and over the ensuing months he became one of the dozens of Japanese military and Kempeitai escapees working for the Nationalist Chinese. At length, on 16 May 1948, Tsuji travelled to Japan disguised as a 'Professor Kenshin Aoki', a classical history don from Peking University. Meanwhile the Allies were trying to trace Tsuji and were slowly tracking down his trail of escape. Although by now the war crimes trials were due to cease, the British were keen to trace Tsuji, have him arrested and charge him with the Singapore massacres.

Unbeknown to the British, Tsuji was to be protected by *Taisa* Takushiro Hattori, who had served with Tsuji in Japan's Kwangtung Army, and who was now working for the Repatriation Agency and with Maj.-Gen. Charles Andrew Willoughby, US Military Intelligence Chief in Occupied Japan. Both saw Tsuji as a key operator in the fight against the Chinese Communists. Even though, as Ian Ward, South East Asia correspondent for the *Daily Telegraph* (1962–87) was to assert, 'Tsuji was the most insidious, calculating, coldly brutal and singularly successful mass killer in the entire Japanese war criminal line up.' Tsuji was now shuttled from safe haven to safe haven in Occupied Japan, and he met up with his former assistant in Singapore *Taisa* Shigeharu Aseada, who was also hiding from Allied authorities dealing with war criminals.

On 1 January 1950 the US officially lifted Tsuji's war criminal status. Tsuji was now safe and boldly published his memoirs as *Underground Escape* (1950). The book brought Tsuji local fame and a positive source of income which he supplemented by working for

Hattori, and more books were to follow. Tsuji now embarked on a political career. He won election to the *Gikai* (Japanese Diet: parliament) as a representative for the Ishikawa 1st District in October 1950 and in 1954 became a founder member of the Liberal Democrat Party.

Tsuji was to fall foul of *Shosho* (Rt) Kiyotake Kawaguchi, who had been angered at Tsuji's assessment of the general in his book *Guadalcanal*. Kawaguchi, who had left the Guadalcanal theatre in the Solomon Islands in disgrace, now prepared an exposure of Tsuji enumerating all the atrocities which he knew Tsuji had organised, including the Singapore Massacres, the infamous Bataan Death March, the slaughter of medical staff and patients at Alexandra Medical Hospital, Singapore, and a long list of atrocities against individuals such as the murder of Philippine Chief Justice José Abad Santos, as well as detailing his associations with and use of the Kempeitai.

Kawaguchi circulated his findings among members of Japan's bi-cameral parliament, underlining how Tsuji had used the Kempeitai to carry out liquidations. Copies of the documents citing Kawaguchi's assertions were received by the UK and US embassies. Worldwide publicity followed Kawaguchi's revelations and Tsuji informed friends that he was going on a six-week tour of South East Asia. He left on 4 April 1961.

Records show that Tsuji was detained by police near Vientiane (Viangchan), the Laotian capital on the north bank of the Mekong River, opposite Thailand. It seems – curiously for an ardent anti-communist – that he was en route to make contact with the North Vietnamese-backed Pathet Lao rebels. It appears, too, that he was seen at Vientiane airport boarding a Russian aircraft for Hanoi. This was on the morning of 10 June 1961; thereafter he vanishes from historical record and was presumed dead on 7 July 1968. In the 1970s stories circulated in Japan that Tsuji had set off to recover Kempeitai gold secreted towards the end of the war. Others averred that he was being held by the Chinese Communists. To add to the mystery surrounding the later life of Masanobu Tsuji there is an empty grave bearing his name at Kannon Jigan Temple, Nozaki, Osaka Prefecture, Japan.

From the Singapore War Crimes Trials in particular comes the case of an officer whose career and crimes were a classic in the Second World War history of the Kempeitai. *Chusa* Haruzo Sumida (*b.* 1903) rose to be chief field officer of the Singapore Branch of *Shosho* (at that time *Taisa*) Masanori Kojima's 3rd Kempeitai, Southern Army. He had joined the Imperial Japanese Army in August 1925 and served first as an artilleryman. In 1935 he was posted as *Tai-i* to the Kempeitai Training School in Tokyo. This led to general Kempeitai duties in Japan and the soon to be Occupied Territories. In May 1943 he was posted to Singapore to play a role in the *Dai Ichi Kosaku* ('Number One Work'), the eradication of anti-Japanese elements which were engaged in sabotage and spreading propaganda damaging to the Japanese war effort.

During the early hours of the morning of 30 September 1943, a huge explosion took place at Singapore port which resulted in the destruction of Japanese cargo boats and oil tankers. On reading the report of the waterfront Kempeitai, Commander of the Southern Army *Taisho* Hisaichi Terauchi ordered the supremo of the 3rd Kempeitai, *Taisa* Kojima, to 'clean up enemy elements in Singapore and in Prai', the latter being the coast of the Malay Peninsula facing Penang Island. For this 'clean up' Kojima ordered Sumida to begin his investigations from his HQ at the former YMCA in Orchard Road. They led to the arrest, interrogation and torture of several residents of Singapore Island including the Rt Revd John Leonard Wilson, Bishop of Singapore, and fifty-seven civilians at Changi Jail.

At length Sumida was sure that the 'leaders of the anti-Japanese elements' were in Changi Jail and that their ringleader was the barrister Robert Heeley Scott CBE, a prominent Foreign Office employee who had been captured in Sumatra. Through the

Chusa *Haruzo Sumida, commander of the Singapore Branch Kempeitai. A career officer in the Kempeitai, he had served in the Kempeitai in China and on mainland Japan. He was found guilty of atrocities at Singapore and was hanged as a war criminal. (William Hodge)*

torturing of Chinese inmates Sumida built up a picture of jail life that the mostly Sikh guards at Changi had never seen – the illegal scams, the information circuits, and the undercover links with civilians outside the jail. Sumida's interrogation of Scott led nowhere and he was handed over to *Heisocho* Tadamori Monai for beatings, torture and further interrogation. Scott revealed nothing, but in the course of interrogation fifteen Changi captives were killed. Scott was tried by the Japanese in a formal court and condemned to six years' imprisonment in Outram Road Jail. These murders were to form the basis of the famous 'Double Tenth Trial' of Sumida and other accused Kempeitai.

Sumida was brought to trial on 18 March 1946 before the Military Court at the Supreme Court Building, Singapore, along with twenty other Kempeitai accused, four of whom were interpreters. The leading member of counsel for the prosecution, Lt-Col. Stuart Colin Sleeman, barrister 16/5th Lancers, and assistant Judge Advocate General HQ Allied Land Forces South East Asia, detailed how Sumida had organised interrogations. Each prisoner had been allotted an NCO for interrogation/torture, with assistance from 'experts in the investigation of particular aspects of the case' (i.e. radio equipment). Details of the harsh conditions in which the prisoners were kept, the course of beatings and torture were related.

Seven areas of Kempeitai ill-treatment were identified: corporal beatings with blunt instruments, belts and revolver butts; the water torture; burning with cigarettes, cheroots, petrol and methylated spirits; electric torture; limb dislocation; psychological tortures (these victims were led to believe they were to be executed forthwith); and threats to wives and families. Tortures were attested by witnesses, as was suffering described as being to 'the limit of human endurance' and to the point of death.

Each of the accused, all of whom pleaded not guilty, were then examined by the court from arraignment on Monday, 18 March to sentencing on Monday, 15 April 1946. The court passed eight

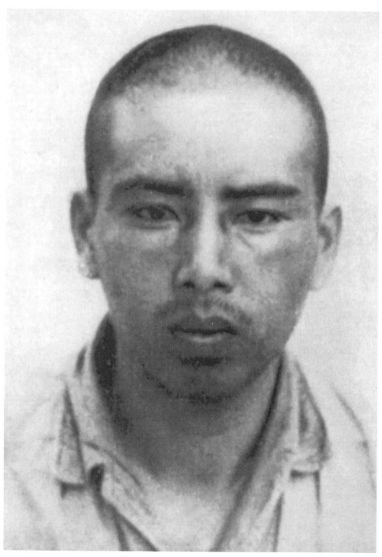

Gunso *Hideo Kasahara, of the 1st Sub-Section, Criminal Section, Singapore Branch Kempeitai. Arresting NCO of PoWs at Changi and of Chinese nationals. Convicted torturer; sentenced to life imprisonment. (William Hodge)*

On the surrender of Singapore on 15 February 1942, some 2,500 civilian prisoners were interned in Changi Prison by the invading Japanese. The numbers had swelled to around 4,000 (a quarter of whom were women and children) by mid-1944. After this date Changi was filled with mostly military PoWs. The Kempeitai regularly raided the prison, abusing its inmates during fatuous searches for radio transmitters and to uncover spy rings.
(William Hodge)

sentences of death, six varying terms of imprisonment and seven acquittals. Robert Scott's torturer *Heisocho* Tadamori Monai was one of those sentenced to death.

The President of the court, Lt-Col. S.C. Silkin, RA, barrister, made an assessment of the character of *Chusa* Haruzo Sumida in such a way that it forms one of the most interesting documents to have entered Kempeitai–related archives. Councils for the defence, advocates Masakaya Hori and Hisakazu Suzuki put forward such a strong case for Sumida's innocence of capital charges that Silkin was constrained to address Sumida in some detail:

> You are a man of education, of intelligence, even in a sense of culture. Yours is the cunning brain under whose direction your instruments of torture performed their evil task. You were well aware of all the moral implications of your policy. In these last six weary years many men have willingly suffered and died in the hope and belief that out of their sacrifice would arise a higher morality in dealings of one nation with another, an international morality soaring above the narrow bonds of patriotism and blind obedience. If, as I believe, some of your victims, Sumida, were amongst those who made their sacrifice in that hope and belief, let this be their epitaph, that they died for an undying cause. To those of us who survive falls the supreme and difficult task of establishing and maintaining that higher morality between nations, of supplanting the rule of force and fear by the rule of law, of ensuring that they did not make their sacrifice in vain.
>
> You, Sumida, have shown by all that you did, ordered and willingly allowed, that to you there is nothing of higher consequence than domination by brute force and fear.
>
> You were prepared, for the glorification, as you thought, of your country, to reduce men and women below the level of beasts and to send them without pity or compunction to an agonizing death. You did not realize that your actions have not glorified, they have degraded, your country. As in the past, so in the future, you would always be the implacable enemy of that great cause for which so many made their sacrifice. You and men like you cannot be allowed to hinder the fulfilment of that cause. Accordingly it is in no spirit of vengeance upon a fallen foe, no desire to have an eye for an eye, a life for a life, that this Court

The courtyard, Changi Prison. Here on 10 October 1943 the Kempeitai paraded and arrested fifty-seven civilians for interrogation. During, or as a consequence of, the interrogation and torture sessions fifteen of the fifty-seven were murdered at Kempeitai HQ. A museum and reconstructed prisoners' chapel is open to the public at Changi. (William Hodge)

has solemnly decided that you must die. Nor is it merely to rid the world — and your country now preparing for its moral rebirth — of one man who is a danger to all moral progress. Rather it is a stern example to all who would willingly support the powers of evil and brute force against the rule of law, justice and humanity.

As time passed the political will to pursue the Kempeitai, and other war criminals, lessened. In Britain Prime Minister Clement Attlee's socialist government wished to re-establish the country's colonial presence and economic clout in the Asian-Pacific region and pulled out of the War Crimes Trials by 1948. Similar post-war plans were being proposed by the Labour government of Joseph Benedict Chifley in Australia and National Party Prime Minister (Sir) Sidney George Holland in New Zealand. On the orders of Democratic Party President Harry S. Truman, MacArthur closed the War Crimes Trials as US long-term naval bases in Japan were planned as a Far Eastern bastion against international communism. Towards this end cooperation was undertaken between Col. Charles Andrew Willoughby, Chief of Allied Intelligence, and second in command to MacArthur, and *Shosho* Seizo Arisue, the head of Japanese military intelligence.

Top secret files which sporadically emerge in the UK and US indicate that ex-Kempeitai personnel served in at least four theatres of war following the Second World War as Allied aides, namely: in the Chinese Civil War, 1945–9; during the Philippines Insurgency, 1946–54; the First Indo-China War, 1946–54; and the Malay Emergency, from 1948. US government documents, declassified in the 1990s, also reveal that Japanese doctors and Kempeitai agents were given secret immunity from prosecution after the war in exchange for their research knowledge concerning the effects of nuclear bombing in Japan and the Japanese secret bacterial warfare programme. The papers revealed that these Japanese were working on this 'research' until 1975, with the intention of building up a file in preparation for future nuclear wars. The 'research' programme was jointly undertaken by CAC (Committee on Atomic Casualties), its successor the ABCC (Atomic Bomb Casualty Commission), and by the Japanese NIH (National Institute of Health) set up by MacArthur in 1947. Emeritus Professor Shingo Shibata of Hiroshima University averred publicly in 1996 that around half of the staff of Japan's IDH (Infectious Diseases Hospital) of the former Imperial Japanese Army Medical College – promoters with the Kempeitai of the bacteriological warfare programme in Manchuquo – were still actively working for the United States in 1983.

With the connivance of the US Occupation Authorities ex-Kempeitai personnel began to appear in the ranks of the re-formed Japanese civilian police force, and soon the career opportunities of ex-Kempeitai were to be re-enhanced. On 25 June 1950 Soviet-equipped communist North Korean troops crossed the 38th Parallel to invade South Korea, and the next day President Truman authorised the US Navy and Air Force to assist South Korean troops. By 8 July MacArthur was named commander of UN troops in South Korea.

Within a few weeks of the outbreak of war, MacArthur instructed that a 75,000-strong National Police Reserve Force be established, and some Western military historians aver that many of the 3,000 Kempeitai still in semi-hiding in the main Japanese island of Honshu obtained positions. Some were just traffic policemen, but nevertheless they had been 'rehabilitated'. The figures for the number within the police ranks remain contentious. By 1952 the *Koan Chosa Cho* (Public Security Investigation Agency), successor to the *Tokushin Kyoku* (Special Investigation Bureau) and in 1954 the *Keibu Bu* (Guard Division) of the *Keisatsu Cho* (Police Agency) were in place, and foreign correspondents speculated on the number of ex-Kempeitai now in what amounted to a Japanese national police and secret service force.

Former Kempeitai personnel were to be harboured, protected, insinuated into society and promoted into postwar commerce and politics by 'Kempeitai Friendship Groups' and Kempeitai Veterans' Associations. An umbrella organisation was formed on 21 March 1953 to coordinate the work of these groups. The organisation is called the *Zenkoku Kenyukai Rengokai* (National Federation of Kempeitai Veterans' Associations) and is known by the acronym

Kempeitai personnel mingle with Imperial Japanese soldiers during a regimental visit to the Yasukuni-jinja – meaning Shrine for Establishing Peace in the Empire – at Kudan Hill, Tokyo. Memorials to the dreaded Kempeitai are displayed here today at what is Japan's foremost war memorial. (Duckworth)

166

ZENKENREN. It is described by the *Nihon Kempei Gaishi* ('The Great History of the Kempeitai', Tokyo 1983) as the 'leading war veterans' group in Japan, with the strongest organisation and best esprit de corps'. By 1985 its membership was some 4,000 and represented 'one third of the former Kempeitai then still alive', according to Nisaku Yoshida, former Kempeitai squad commander in Changzhou, China, then president of the Toko Printing Co., Tokyo.

The ZENKENREN has a four-fold intention: to 'affirm the value of the Kempeitai'; to keep alive the memory of the Kempeitai war dead; to promote friendship and fellowship among those Kempeitai still alive and their families; to aid in every way possible the dependants of those Kempeitai lost in the war.

On 28 May 1959, Emperor Hirohito gave an order in person to the Shinto priests who administer the *Yasukuni-jinja* to inscribe the names of all Japan's war criminals on to the scrolls of the 2,500,000 immortal military dead commemorated at the shrine. After the formal order had been made he and Empress Nagako prayed for the souls of the war criminals at a private shrine set to the rear of the main temple and reserved for bereaved relatives of the war dead. Then he addressed the widows and relatives of the Japanese war criminals who form 'The Society of the White Chrysanthemum'.

The *Koe no Tsuru* was heard to utter words which were deemed blasphemous to the memories of the thousands of dead PoWs: 'I HAVE A SPECIAL APPRECIATION FOR THE FAMILIES OF OUR WAR CRIMINALS. I KNOW WHAT THEY HAVE DONE FOR JAPAN. THEY WERE AMONG OUR GREATEST LEADERS.' Ten years later the ZENKENREN set up a small memorial to the Kempeitai war dead in a quiet wooded corner of the *Yasukuni-jinja*. It honours the souls and spirits of the Kempeitai; yet, ironically, it is a permanent reminder of their infamy.

GLOSSARY

Pronunciation stress-marks have been omitted and the *Romaji* (Romanisation; transliteration) of Japanese terms and vocabulary follows the Modified Japanese Language System of US medical missionary the Revd Dr James Curtis Hepburn (1815–1911). Where Japanese persons are mentioned in the text, given name then surname are set out, as in the Western style. This section includes background notes on Japanese terms and Kempeitai colloquial vocabulary used in the text.

Aeso Japanese guard house

Aikokushin Patriotic nationalism

Asahi Shimbun One of the five prominent national newspapers

Banzai ('May the Emperor live for) 10,000 years'. Battlecry; salute; exclamation of joy

Bentatsu The everyday striking, punching or beating of soldiers to underline orders given. In Japan's military code it was carried out as *shinsetsu-na okonai* (an act of kindness). In the Imperial Japanese Navy the bashings were called *tekken/seisai* (the iron fist) delivered as the *ai-no-muchi* (whip of love). Slapping of PoWs was thus a common occurrence

Bogyaku A state of tyranny

Bunkentai (Army) detachments

Buntai (Army) sections

Burakumin Class of untouchables

Bushido 'The Way of the Warrior'. A code of honour on which every *samurai* (warrior) was expected to base his conduct

Chian Ije (Police) maintenance of order

Chian Ije Ho Peace Preservation Law
Chiji Governor
Chosen Japanese name for Korea; annexed in 1910
Chosen Sotoku Fu Government General of Korea
Chu-i Rank: Army, 1st Lt; Navy, Sub-Lieutenant
Chujo Rank: Army, Lt-Gen.; Navy, Vice-Admiral
Chusa Rank: Army, Lt-Col.; Navy, Commander
Dai-A-Gi-Kai 'Re-Awakening of Greater Asia Society'
Daihonei Imperial General HQ
Daikan Local police intendants
Daimyo Feudal lords
Dai ni-ji Sekai Taisen Second World War
Dai Nippon (or Nihon) Great Japan
Dai Nippon Teikoku Empire of Great Japan
Dai Nippon Teikoku Kaigun Imperial Japanese Navy
Dai Nippon Teikoku Rikugun Imperial Japanese Army
Dai Toa Kyozonken 'Great East Asia Co-existence Sphere' Japanese slogan; euphemism for their occupied territories from Manchuquo to the Dutch East Indies; policy under the guise of a politically and economically integrated Asia 'free from Western domination'
Dai Toa Sen 'Great East Asia War'; Japanese term for Second World War
Danshaku Title: Baron
Domei Japanese News Agency
Doshin Early foot-patrol police
Furyo PoWs
Furyo shuyojo PoW camps
Gaijin Foreigner
Gaimu-daijin Foreign Minister
Gaimusho Foreign Office
Genki nada Strip of water between Japanese main island of Kyushu and Korea
Gensui Rank: Army, Field Marshal; Navy, Admiral of the Fleet

Genyosha 'Black Ocean Society'; former *Kayosha* National Assembly pressure groups, 1881

Gocho Rank: Army, corporal

Goningumi 'Five-family associations'; collective responsibility groups

Gumi Families, term used by *yakusa* (*q.v.*)

Gumpo kaigi Court-martial; comparable with western practice

Gunji himitsu Military secrets

Gunritsu kaigi Trial of civilians by military court

Gunso Rank: Army, Sgt

Gyokusai Armageddon; the act of seeking death rather than dishonour

Gyosei Keisatsu Kisoku Administrative Police Regulation

Hakko Ichiu 'The Whole World Under One Rule'; Japanese national sentiment for Occupied Territories

Hakushaku Title: Count

Heimu Kyoku Military Administration Bureau

Heisocho Rank: Warrant Officer

Hikari Kaikan Civil intelligence and sabotage organisation

Himitsu kessha Secret societies

Hinomaru 'Round of the Sun', Japanese national flag. During Second World War the Army and Navy used a flag which had the Rising Sun red rays on a white background

Homengun shireibu Area Army HQ

Homusho Second, and later, name of the Ministry of Justice

Ianjo Army 'Comfort House' (i.e., brothel); Navy equivalent *Kaigun ianjo*

Ittohei Rank: 1st Class Privates

Jiken Rikugun-daijin Vice-Minister of War

Jitte Short metal truncheon carried by low-ranking policemen

Joho Information/intelligence

Joho-kikan Army Intelligence Service

Jotohei Rank: Superior Privates

Jugun ianfu 'Comfort women'; usually Asiatic women forced into prostitution for Japanese servicemen

Junshikan Rank: Warrant Officer
Kaigun-daijin Navy Minister
Kaigun Heigako Navy Academy
Kami Japan's pantheon of gods
Kamishibai Paper-picture show (for children)
Kanshi-hei (Camp) guards; usually a rank given to Koreans, Sikhs and Formosans
Karafuto Colonial administration of Southern Sakhalin, islands now within the Russian Far East. It was Japanese colonial policy to have a Kempeitai presence from day one of their administration, and to remain as long as required. In the case of Karafuto, where there was a 95 per cent ethnic Japanese population, they had only a two-year presence, 1905–7
Karayuki Travelling prostitutes, usually Japanese nationals
Kashikan Rank: NCOs
Kebiishi Ancient Police Department of Japan
Keibitei Mixture of regular Kempeitai officers and auxiliaries; units particularly used at Singapore
Keibu Bu Police Agency
Keihokyoku Police Bureau
Keikan Policeman
Keimu Hon Sub-section of Kempeitai
Keimukyoku Police Affairs Department
Keisatsu (Cho) Modern Japanese Police Force
Keishicho Tokyo Metropolitan Police Department
Kempei Keisatsu Gendarmerie operating in Korea
Ken Japanese prefectures
Ketsumeidan 'Blood Brotherhood'; right-wing anarchist movement
Kikosaku Severe punishment without martial law intervention, leading to execution; a Kempeitai concept of policing
Koan Chosa Cho Public Security Investigation Agency, 1952
Kodoshugisha 'Japan's Imperial Way' (of doing things)
Koe No Tsuru 'Voice of the Crane'; euphemism for the sacred

voice of the Emperor. The Japanese crane is the symbol of the Emperor or the Imperial Throne. An old Japanese saying noted that even though the crane was out of sight its call would always be heard

Koho Kimmu Yoin Yoseijo   'Rear Service Personnel Training Centre'; established in 1938 at Kudan (moved to Nakaro, 1940), Tokyo. Operated 1938–41 the secret intelligence programme called RIKUGUN NAKANO GAKKO

Kokubo Hoan Ho   National Defence Security Law

Kokumin Seishin Sodoin Remmei   League for the Mobilisation of the Peoples' Spirit; active in Korea

Kokumin Seishin Sodoin Undo   National Spiritual Mobilisation Movement

Kokuryukai   'Black Dragon Society'

Koshaku   Title: Prince

Kyokuto Kokusai Gunji Saiban   International Military Tribunal for the Far East

Kyujo   Imperial Palace, Tokyo

Machi bugyo   Town magistrates

Mainichi Shimbun   National daily newspaper of 'progressive views', founded 1872

Manchuquo   Japanese name for Manchuria; modern Dongbei, China. From 1931 to 1945 the provinces of modern Heilongjiang, Jilin and Liaoning constituted a Japanese puppet state. Many Kempeitai achieved their field experience here

Manshu Jiken   Manchurian Incident, 18 September 1931

Maruta   Logs; Kempeitai jargon for prisoners for the human experiments programme

Meakashi   Early police detectives; many of dubious character

Metsuke   Police inspectors

Mombusho   Ministry of Education

Naikin Han   Administrative sub-sections of the Kempeitai

Naimusho   Home Ministry

Nan'yo-cho   South Seas (Occupation) Government; Micronesia

Nihon Ginko Bank of Japan
Nihon Hoso Kyokai NHK – Japanese Broadcasting Corporation
Nihon Kofuku Bunsho Japan's Instrument of Surrender
Nihon Koku State of Japan
Ninja 'invisible agents'
Nippon Ryojikan Japanese consulate
Nisei Persons of Japanese parentage born in US territories
Nitohei Rank· Army, 2nd Class Privates
Niwanban Gardeners of the Shogunate, used as spies
Okura-daijin Minister of Finance
Ommitsu Secret agents
Rikugun Daigako Army General Staff College
Rikugun-daijin Minister of War
Rikugun Shikan Gakko Military Academy
Rikugunsho Ministry of War
Rikugun Yasen Gakko Military preparatory schools
Roju Senior administrators
Ronin Masterless *samurai* who hired themselves out as swordsmen in feudal Japan
Ryoji Consul
Sakan Field Officer
Sambo Hombu Imperial General Staff
Samurai Medieval Japanese warriors; third level of Japanese social class
Seiyukai Rural/agrarian bourgeois political party. Evolved in the 1920s
Senso Hanzai War Crime
Seppuku Ritual disembowelment; the polite term instead of the vulgar *hara-kiri*. Japan's aristocracy was the only one to evolve a highly ritualised method of committing suicide. It underlined the *Bushido* code of 'Victory or Death'.
Seto Naikai 'Inland Sea'; part of the Pacific Ocean between the Japanese main island of Honshu to the north and east and the southerly main islands of Shikoku and Kyushu

Shihisho Ministry of Justice
Shinjuwan Kogeki Assault on Pearl Harbor
Shocho Rank: Army, Sgt-Major
Shogun Japanese generalissimos who exerted almost unlimited powers in medieval Japan in the name of puppet emperors. Hereditary *Shogun* ruled Japan from the twelfth century to 1867.
Sho-i Rank: Army, 2nd Lt; Navy, Sub-Lt (Acting)
Shoko-daijin Minister of Commerce and Industry
Shonan 'The Radiant South'; Japanese-occupied Singapore
Shosa Rank: Army, Major; Navy, Lt-Cdr
Shosho Rank: Army, Maj-Gen.; Navy, Rear-Admiral
Shukai jorei Public meetings
Shukusei Purge
Socho Rank: Army, Sgt-Major
Sori-daijin Prime Minister
Soshi 'Brave Knights'; unemployed *samurai* out to make mischief
Tai-i Rank: Army, Captain; Navy, 1st Lt
Taisa Rank: Army, Col.; Navy, Captain
Taishi Ambassador
Taisho Rank: Army, General; Navy, Admiral
Teikoku Daigaku Imperial University, Tokyo
Teishinsho Communications Ministry
Tenko PoW camp roll-call
Tenno The Emperor: *Tenno Banzai* – colloquial: 'Long Live the Emperor'
Tenyukyo Society of the Celestial Salvation of the Oppressed; subsidiary group of the secret society, the *Genyosha*
Toa Shinchitsujo New Order of Asia (with Japan as leader)
Tokei-tai Naval Secret Police
Tokubetsu Gumpo Kaiji Court-martial wherein the defendant is granted no legal representation or appeal
Tokubetsu Koto Keisatsu TOKKO – Special Service 'Thought Police'
Tokumu Han Special Service Kempeitai

Tokumu Kaikan   Special Service Agency (Military Intelligence)
Tokushin Kyoku   Special Investigation Bureau
Tonari Gumi   Neighbourhood Association
Tsuyaku   Interpreter
Wakadoshiyori   Junior councillors
Yakusa   Japanese Mafia
Yasen Kempeitai   Numbered field units
Yasukuni-jinja   Yasukuni Shrine – nation's main war memorial
Yoriki   Early mounted police
Yudaya-jin   Jews
Zenkoku Kenyukai Rengokai   Acronym: ZENKENREN, 'National Federation of Kempeitai Veterans' Associations'

BIBLIOGRAPHY

There are a number of books in Japanese on various aspects of the Kempeitai; below are a representative sample of primary sources:

Nihon Kenpei Seishi 'The Authentic History of the Kempeitai' (Tokyo, 1976), by Zenkoku Kenyukai Rengokai Honbu on behalf of Zenkoku Kenyukai Rengokai Hensan, 'The Editorial Committee of the National Federation of Kempeitai Veterans' Associations'.

Nihon Kenpei Gaishi 'The General History of the Kempeitai' (Tokyo, 1983).

Junkoku Kenpei no Isho 'Last Testaments of Kempeitai Who Died for their Country' (Tokyo, 1982).

It should be remembered that these volumes, based on interviews with former Kempeitai soldiers, their diaries and letters, depict the Kempeitai war dead not as criminals but as martyrs who were sacrificed for the glory of Japan.

Showa Ki No Kempeitai Shi 'A History of the Kempeitai in the Showa Era' (Tokyo 1966), by Keijiro Otani.

For material on the Kempeitai in Occupied Territories the following are good primary sources:

Syjuco, Maria Felisa A. *The Kempeitai in the Philippines, 1941–45.* New Day Publishers, Quezon City, Philippines, 1988.

Del Rio, Benigno *Siete Días en el Infierno: En Manos de la Gestapo Nipona* ('Seven Days in Hell: In the Hands of the Nipponese Gestapo'), Philippines, 1945.

Reyes, Jose G. *Terrorism and Redemption: Japanese Atrocities in the Philippines*, Philippines, 1946.

Shimer, Barbara Gifford and Hobbs, Guy, *The Kempeitai in Java and Sumatra*, Cornell Modern Indonesia Project, Cornell University Press, 1986.

General Sources

Allbury, A.G. *Bamboo and Bushido*, Robert Hale, 1955.

Argall, Phyllis, *Prisoner in Japan*, Geoffrey Bles, 1945.

Browne, Courtney, *Tojo: The Last Banzai*, Angus & Robertson, 1967.

Bryan, J. Ingram, *Japanese All*, Methuen, 1928.

Butow, Robert, J.C. *Tojo and the Coming War*, Princeton University Press, 1961.

Carr, William, *Poland to Pearl Harbor*, Edward Arnold, 1985.

Craigie, Sir Robert, *Behind the Japanese Mask*, Hutchinson, 1945.

Daws, Gavan, *Prisoners of the Japanese: PoWs of the Second World War in the Pacific – the Powerful Untold Story*, Robson Books, 1994.

Deacon, Richard, *Kempeitai: The Japanese Secret Service Then and Now*, Charles E. Tuttle, Tokyo, 1990.

Deakin, F.W. and Storry, G.R., *The Case of Richard Sorge*, Chatto & Windus, 1966.

Duus, Masayu, *Tokyo Rose: Orphan of the Pacific*, Kodansha, 1979.

Foot, M.R.D., and Langley, J.M., *MI–9 Escape and Evasion 1939–1945*, Bodley Head, 1979.

Fuller, Richard, *Shokan: Hirohito's Samurai – Leaders of the Japanese Armed Forces, 1926–1945*, Arms & Armour Press, 1992.

Fujiwara, Iwaichi, *F Kikan: Japanese Army Intelligence Operations in Southeast Asia During World War II*, Heinemann Asia, 1983.

Gold, Hal, *Unit 731: Japan's Wartime Human Experimentation Programme*, Yen Books, 1986.

Hanayama, Shinsho, *The Way of Deliverance: Three Years with the Condemned Japanese War Criminals*, Victor Gollancz, 1955.

BIBLIOGRAPHY

Hicks, George, *Comfort Women: Sex Slaves of the Japanese Imperial Forces*, Souvenir Press, 1995.

Johnson, Chalmers, *An Instance of Treason: The Story of the Tokyo Spy Ring*, Heinemann, 1965.

Lamont-Brown, Raymond, *Kamikaze: Japan's Suicide Samurai*, Arms & Armour Press, 1997.

Lichauco, Marcial P., *Dear Mother Putnam: a Diary of War in the Philippines*, Manila, 1949.

McKale, Donald M., *The Swastika Outside Germany*, Kent State University Press, Ohio, 1977

Mackay, James, *Betrayal in High Places*, Tasman Archives, New Zealand, 1996.

Meo, L. D., *Japan Radio War on Australia 1941–45*, Melbourne University Press, 1968.

Morris, John, *Traveller from Tokyo*, Cresset Press, 1943.

Russell of Liverpool, Lord, *The Knights of the Bushido: The Shocking History of the Japanese War Atrocities*, Cassell, 1958.

Schellenburg, Walter, *The Schellenburg Memoirs*, Andre Deutsch, 1956.

Seth, Ronald, *Secret Servants: A History of Japanese Espionage*, Victor Gollancz, 1957.

Sleeman, Colin, and Silkin, S.C. (eds), *The Double Tenth Trial*, William Hodge, 1951.

Tanaka, Yuki, *Hidden Horrors: Japanese War Crimes in World War II*, Westview Press, 1996.

Tokayer, Marvin, and Swartz, Mary, *The Fugu Plan: The Untold Story of the Japanese and the Jews During World War II*, Paddington Press, 1979.

Tolischus, Otto David, *Tokyo Record*, Hamish Hamilton, 1943.

US War Department, *Handbook on Japanese Military Forces*, Louisiana State University Press, 1995.

Vespa, Amleto, *Secret Agent of Japan*, Victor Gollancz, 1938.

Ward, Ian, *The Killer They Called a God*, Media Masters, Singapore, 1993.

Whitecross, R.H., *Slaves of the Son of Heaven*, Dymock's Book Arcade, Sydney, 1952.

INDEX